Raise Your Vibration

Awaken to Your Highest Soul's Potential

by

Sabrina Reber

About the Author

Sabrina Reber resides in Destin Florida with her husband Todd and her two children Alexandrea and Savannah. Sabrina is a Mother, Artist, Author, Ordained Minister in the Lively Stones Healing Ministry, Reiki Master Teacher & Healer and a Karuna Healing Practitioner. In 2005, after a two-year "Dark Night of the Soul," she experienced a spontaneous Spiritual Awakening that transformed her life and way of "Being" in the world. She was placed on a path of rapid healing and transformation, which opened her up to her Soul's Mission on Earth at this time. The information, tools and techniques Sabrina shares in this book are from her own personal experience of raising her vibration and are also used by many others on their journey back to wholeness.

The cover of this book was designed by Sabrina and is symbolic of a Divine Enlightened Human with an activated chakra system grounding its divine energy into the Earth so it can fulfill its divine mission and highest soul's potential as a Christed Human Angel on Earth at this time.

For more information please visit:
www.Raiseyourvibration.com

Contents

Our Highest Soul's Potential

We live in a time of accelerated change and transformation. There are many names for this time period. Some call it: The Great Awakening, The Rebirth, The New Earth, The Second Coming, The Golden Age, The End Times, The New Millennium, The Age of Aquarius, The Return of Christ, The Rapture, The Apocalypse, Armageddon, The Quickening or Planetary Ascension. Regardless of what you call it, it is happening and it is happening now. We are entering the most intensified purification process the Earth and humanity has ever experienced. Our world is set to transform.

According to many legends, writings and prophecies - 2012 is a year of extraordinary importance. It is believed that the Mayan calendar ends on December 21, 2012 with the Earth aligned in the center, or galactic heart, of the Milky Way. This is a cyclic event that occurs every 26,000 years as the Earth completes a full revolution around the sun. In 13,000-year cycles the Earth spends 11,000 years - in the darkness of separation and duality- *outside* the light of the photon band. The photon band is a band of high vibrational intensified light that comes from the great central sun. Currently, the Earth is moving into a 2000-year period of transformational energies moving *inside* the photon band where humanity's next level of advancement is offered. While we are in the photon band, encodings activating our memory and DNA are sent through the rays of the sun encouraging us to spiritually evolve going beyond our current state of consciousness to a more enlightened state of being. For the past 11,000 years we have been outside the photon belt in the dark ages immersed in the negativity of polarity and duality. Currently, we are in the photon belt, entering a 2,000- year cycle of en-lighten-ment receiving the transformational and transmutational energies of the Christ.

The return of Christ is the return of our Christ Consciousness, which is activated by the photon belt. The photon belt is the radiation and eminence of the Christ energy, which awakens humanity and ushers in the era of peace. This is the time of separating the wheat from the chaff. Humanity at this time has a choice to remain just as they are refusing to grow and expand their current level of being or we can choose to actively participate in our soul's transformational process fully accepting and integrating the incoming energies of the Christ Consciousness. This is a personal choice where we choose through our own free will to no longer experience the negativity of 3rd dimensional darkness and choose to transform the density of our being into a light being where we put on our garments of light ascending into the higher vibrations of full consciousness, unity consciousness, unconditional love, peace, joy, harmony, spiritual abundance, health and healing.

The divine plan is unfolding and the Earth and all beings, who choose, are rising in vibration and accepting the transformational energies of the Christ. This process has nothing to do with religion! It has everything to do with the level of our frequency or vibration and our desire to transform our current level of being into a more light filled one. The Christed energies of the photon belt will dismantle the existing 3rd dimensional structures and organizations residing in the lower vibrations of fear, control, separation and the human ego creating space for something new and more divinely aligned to be created. Humans are part of the Earth and because the Earth is moving into the very high vibrational light of the photon belt, we also must rise in vibration and begin our own process of cleansing, releasing and healing. Your soul and spiritual self are urging you to shake off your old distorted beliefs and lack of knowledge from the dark ages. It is time to step into the light of knowledge seeking en-lighten-ment removing the layers of illusion based on fear and separation releasing everything that no longer serves your highest good. It is time for you to **AWAKEN** and to remember who you are and why you are here allowing yourself to fully embody the power of your very own Christ Consciousness. Each of us are divinely guided by a higher intelligence, if you are reading this book your God self has led you here. It is time for you to awaken and to break the chains that have held you down. It is time for you to raise your vibration and become an active conscious participant in the creation of the New Earth.

Raising your Vibration

What is your vibration? Your vibration is your personal energy frequency. It is a culmination of every life you have ever lived, every thought you have ever had and every action you have ever performed. It is the energy that surrounds and permeates every cell in your body. Your vibration is your divine signature, your soul essence, and it is special only to you. Just as there are no two snowflakes alike, no two souls in the entire universe have the same name or "soul signature". That's how incredibly unique and special you are. Your vibration is a direct reflection of your inner thoughts, feelings, beliefs, choice of words, how well you take care of yourself, the Earth and others. The higher your vibration the more light you hold, the faster your light particles vibrate, the higher your consciousness and the stronger you are connected to your soul and God self.

When your vibration is low, your light particles are vibrating slowly and become condensed. Your energy literally feels heavy because you are not in alignment with your soul or divine self and are mostly operating from your lower self or ego. Distorted beliefs, fear, anger, resentment, blame, guilt, jealousy, judgment, shame, addiction, unforgiveness, conditional love, lack of self worth, greed, separation consciousness and poor health keep you in very dense low vibrating energy. When you are a high vibrational being you recognize your divinity and the divinity within others. You are in alignment with your soul, which is nourished by spirit, you are vibrantly healthy and your life flows with ease and grace.

Although we identify ourselves with our physical body we are actually energy or light beings. EVERYTHING IS ENERGY. Every thought, word, feeling and thing is energy….everything! Things that appear to be solid are actually very tightly compacted energy particles creating a shape, form or physical matter. Our physical body, that part of us that is not eternal, is surrounded by our eternal divine essence consisting of our emotional, mental and spiritual energetic layers. We are much more than our physical body; we are actually multidimensional, energetic, spiritual beings having a physical human experience. It is important for us to bring into our awareness the many layers of our energetic body. This is the key to our self-empowerment. When it is brought into our awareness, our soul will begin to integrate all of the layers of ourselves bringing us into a state of wholeness. Each of us needs to become aware of who we really are and reclaim all of our energy.

When we become aware of our energetic bodies and set our intention to heal, balance and activate them, we have the potential to raise our vibration to such a point that each layer of our energetic body will unify and activate the creation of our "light body". When this occurs we have reached a very high vibrational state where our spiritual self or God self is able to merge with our physical body. This cannot occur until we have raised our vibration high enough for divine union to occur. This is the moment of en-lighten-ment and the return to one's true spiritual essence and identity. Once this occurs, we will never be the same and we will be propelled forward beginning a new more evolved journey into self-mastery and the development of our Christ Consciousness. This is the true meaning of being "reborn". We reincarnate ourselves while in a physical body. Being reborn is a physical, energetic, blissful experience. Being reborn is not a mental concept, a belief or a desire to be a better person. It is an incredible experience where every cell in our body is flooded with light, all of our energetic fields and chakras are cleared, energetic blocks and karma is released, dormant strands of DNA are activated, our spiritual gifts are returned and our consciousness is expanded.

Being reborn is when our divine essence or God self merges with our physical body and we experience complete oneness with God and all beings. We experience our true nature, the truth of our being, which will catapult us into a new journey of self-transcendence. This is divine plan for everyone to eventually reach this state of divine union helping us to bring Heaven (Spirit) here down on Earth (Matter).

We are in the process of planetary ascension and everyone choosing to stay on this planet will raise their vibration high enough to anchor in their Spiritual self or God self. Each of us are being asked to surrender to this process allowing ourselves to be "reborn" shedding the illusions of the ego and shining light on our shadow consciousness so we can bring all of our disowned rejected parts of ourselves into wholeness. Although our spiritual self is never separated from us it does reside in a higher vibrating dimension, several feet above our head, called the spiritual realm. The Creator has given us free will and it must be our choice to choose to climb the mountain of self in order to access and activate our divine birthright of God realization. This is divine plan and bringing our higher vibrating, loving, true selves down into our physical body is how we will heal the planet. Expecting someone or something outside of ourselves to save us is disempowering and will not get us anywhere. No one is going to save us; we have to save ourselves. We have to heal ourselves and we have to heal the planet. We have to take personal responsibility for our own vibration and salvation. We cannot give our power away anymore to the churches, the governments, the healthcare system or the financial system. Your power to change resides in yourself. You must commit to your own soul growth and spiritual development and shift your focus from trying to accomplish "things" to devotion and connection with your God self.

The mass consciousness of the planet is being bathed in high vibrational photon energy emitted from the galactic center, sun and stars. This energy is shaking our foundation, penetrating every cell in our bodies and triggering our DNA codes awakening us to our true magnificence. This very high vibrational light energy is a gift from God encouraging us to transform our denseness. Unfortunately, many people are so engulfed in the physical illusion and are vibrating at such a low rate; they are having a hard time adjusting to these higher vibrational frequencies. They are unaware of what is happening and are resisting the process of transformation and change doing everything they can to avoid the inner work necessary to raise their vibration. Anxiety, chaos, drama, war, confusion, anger, stress, rage and erratic behavior are all symptomatic of humanity's resistance to receiving this divine light. The chaos of the world is a reflection of our own inner chaos. It's not that we have more darkness on the planet, it's that we have more light permeating the planet forcing the darkness *within each of us* to rise to the surface to be healed, transmuted and released. Each of us are going through a period of spiritual detox and investing in our spiritual self and making a conscious decision to actively participate in the raising of our own personal vibration will assist us in moving through this time period with ease and grace. Where we focus our energy is precious! If we focus our energy on spiritual development and emotional clearing we will rise in vibration and expand our consciousness. After all, it is our state of consciousness that creates our world. Expanding our consciousness goes hand and hand with raising our vibration and it needs to be our top priority if we want to enter into the Golden Age. There are many ways to raise our vibration. The most important thing we can do right now is state our intention.

"I AM READY TO RAISE MY VIBRATION INTEGRATING THE ENERGIES OF THE CHRIST CONSCIOUSNESS INTO MY BEING WITH EASE AND GRACE AND FOR MY HIGHEST GOOD "

The universe always follows your command and you will be amazed how quickly things start shifting for you. Please be aware that the Great Awakening is happening in large groups of people one wave at a time. If it did not happen in stages, our planet would be in total upheaval! The first and second wave have already occurred and these beings are helping to awaken those in the third and fourth waves which will culminate on December 21, 2012 and beyond. Although I will discuss countless ways for you to raise your vibration, stating your intention **EVERYDAY**, shifting your thoughts and beliefs, getting in touch with your feelings, releasing toxic emotions, integrating the ego, overcoming shadow consciousness, as well as, daily **MEDITATION** are the most important things you can do.

Faster vibrations mean getting closer to Spirit. Slower vibrations keep us in the world of problems.

Wayne Dyer

The vibration, the rate of speed, the wavelength, the frequency of your emanations shift and change constantly with your thoughts, mood, feelings, words and actions. And so, the ether, the air between you is filled with energy. It is the collective consciousness, the vibrational frequency of all beings affecting everything on your planet.

Neale Donald Walsh

Accepting Yourself

In order to begin the process of raising your vibration it is necessary for you to accept yourself right here, right now, just as you are. Everyone on the planet is coming out of the dark ages and has the opportunity to change their previous way of living and thinking into a more enlightened, compassionate way of being. All of us have done things in the past we regret doing. It is karmic law when a person chooses to acknowledge their misqualified energy and has chosen to transcend the potential of repeating a negative karmic behavior the energetic imprint of that behavior is released and all is forgiven. Regardless of what has occurred in the past or what is occurring in the present moment, if you don't accept yourself and love yourself right now you will not be able to shift your current state of vibration into a higher one, so you can manifest a higher vibrational you in the future.

Our Creator DOES NOT judge us for our actions or our choices! We are loved **unconditionally!** Unconditional love is an **unlimited** way of being! Our Creator loves us so much he gave us free will, with **no limitations**, to choose how we want to create with his energy. However, all of our choices and actions reflect the level of our vibration and state of consciousness. Since you are reading this book, clearly you desire to change your current state of consciousness into a higher state of consciousness where you can create a more harmonious life for yourself and everyone you come in contact with. This can only occur through a gradual process of integrating your Spiritual self or God self with your physical body. A relationship with your God self will assist your soul in gaining right understanding helping you to avoid making self destructive or limiting choices in the future.

Your Spiritual self or God self is the core of your being and is completely pure and unaffected by any of the energies in the physical dimension. Nothing you have ever done has corrupted or changed the core essence of your being. Your God self, a direct extension of the Creator, lives in a higher octave and is completely whole and never separated from you or the Creator of All That Is. The Creator took of his light and created your God Self and your God Self took a part of its consciousness creating the soul where it extended itself into the earth plane taking on a physical body. As a newborn child, the soul enters the body and a veil of amnesia or forgetfulness is placed over the soul's mind and the soul forgets that it is an extension of the Creator. Because the soul believes it is separated and powerless, it becomes fearful and creates an alter identity called the Ego or the lower self. **The Ego is a fear filled extension of the soul and is not connected to the loving guidance of the God self.** Out of desperation and confusion the soul allows the Ego to become the dominating source of guidance which creates blocks and barriers between the soul and its true source of wisdom and guidance, the God self. The Ego is an acronym for **E**dging **G**od **O**ut and once it is in control of the soul, it will do everything to keep the soul from remembering its true nature. Because the soul has free will, the God Self will allow the soul and its self-created alter identity the ego, to experience its free will to the fullest. The God self is a source of wisdom and guidance but it does not intervene in the soul's free will if the soul chooses to follow the guidance of the Ego.

Humanity has been in a dualistic battle with its ego for the past 11,000 years. Since we are moving into the photon belt of Christed energies and out of the 11,000 years of darkness it is time for each of us to remember who we truly are releasing the control, lies and fears of our Ego or lower self. It is time for our soul to step back into alignment so we can be spiritually fed and guided by the love of our God self. In order for the soul to access divine guidance it must, choose for itself, to take dominion over its ego. The soul needs to release the control of ego separation reclaiming its soul presence and divine birthright to fully merge into sacred union with its God self. This can only occur if the soul chooses to release the belief that it is separated from its Creator and actively pursues divine union with its God self through the process of raising its vibration, expanding its consciousness and seeking the kingdom within.

Your soul has free will and may have made poor choices in the past based on fear, however, deep inside of you there is a place of perfection and divine wisdom. The purpose of this book and all spiritual work is to get you to strengthen that connection with your God self so you can receive an unlimited amount of divine energy leading you into self empowerment and your highest soul's potential. Everything in your life revolves around the free will choices of your soul. Your God self will not make choices for your soul but it is always available if your soul chooses to be guided by its divine wisdom and higher intelligence. However, it is the soul who has chosen to incarnate into a physical body and has the free will to choose whether it wants to make choices from the ego or the God self.

The shifting of your vibration begins when you accept responsibility for all of your perceived faults, mistakes, regrets, difficulties and challenges. You cannot deny the choices your soul has made in the past but you can change the present moment and your future by reviewing your past actions, unconscious choices and egoic beliefs. Self-analysis and observation is the only way you can create change in your life. Forgive yourself and know that all of your previous actions were created from your level of consciousness at that time in your life. However, it is imperative that you understand that your current problems cannot be solved with the same state of consciousness that created them. Be honest with yourself, love yourself, open yourself up to a higher perspective and allow a shift in consciousness to occur. You are not your mistakes! You are a powerful being fully capable of creating the life you have always wanted.

You are created in the image and likeness of God. You are created from source energy and have the same energy within you that is also within the Creator. Underneath all of the pain, sadness, masks, shields of protection, denials, distorted beliefs and limitations is a perfect eternal divine spark that can never be extinguished. This is your God spark, your perfection, the part of you that is a divine extension of God. You have within you God power that can heal and create the change you desire to see in your life. Jesus says, "The power that is within you is greater than the power that is in this world." You are a co-creator with God! You have God essence, God power within your being. Many of us have become so consumed with our physicality and ego, we forgot about our true identity as a spiritual being and stopped using our creative powers consciously. This has caused us to make unconscious choices creating suffering for humanity, the planet and ourselves. God does not create suffering; humans create suffering! We are spiritual beings having a human experience and we have forgotten how powerful we are. In fact, we are so powerful, we have the free will potential to use our creative faculties in a way that goes *against* God's laws creating great disharmony on our planet.

There is not a person here on Earth who has not made mistakes in the past. Mistakes are misqualified energy and are opportunities for growth. Through the pain and suffering of human mistakes our greatest lessons and soul growth can be attained. However, we must become conscious of our mistakes and gain the golden nuggets of wisdom they are trying to teach us. Being observant of ourselves shifts our consciousness into a higher state so we can rise above our past choices and repetitive patterns that continue to lead us into suffering, lower vibrations and ultimately a very thick veil of illusion, created by our ego, making it appear that we are separated from God and each other. The good news is we can choose to reverse our downward spiral right here, right now that moves our soul further and further away from our God selves into an upward spiral bringing us closer to our divine essence. We need to step out of denial and acknowledge our errors. Victim consciousness and denial of our unconscious choices will get us nowhere. We can't change anything if we don't first acknowledge it! Accept where you are right here, right now and know you have the power within you to make new choices that will expand your consciousness moving you into an upward spiral where you have the potential to raise your vibration high enough so you can attain divine union with your God self.

The human you is imperfect but the true you, the eternal you, your spiritual self, is whole and perfect. It is your soul, your consciousness, that desires healing and a stronger connection to your Spiritual or God self. Many of us have allowed our egos or lower selves to take over pushing our souls, that part of ourselves that is always connected to the God self, out of the way. Although we have never been separated from our God self, many of us have chosen to believe in the concept of God being outside of ourselves. This is an egoic belief! Unfortunately, this belief creates energetic blocks and barriers between our physical and spiritual selves creating the illusion that we are separated from God and each other. When we believe we are separate from God, the flow of spiritual energy and wisdom from our God selves diminishes to a small trickle barely keeping us alive. A limited flow of spiritual energy depletes the soul leading to poor health, distorted beliefs, confusion, depression, powerlessness, shame, anger and negative choices that are out of alignment with our higher wisdom. The soul is always trying to get our attention by communicating to us through feelings and oftentimes through pain in the physical body. The chaos on our planet is the effect of the mass consciousness choosing to unplug themselves from the higher wisdom of their God selves. We have allowed our egos and lower selves to make decisions for us leading all of us into a downward spiral of self-destruction.

When Jesus says, " I am the way and the only way to my Father" he is acknowledging that only through HIMSELF can he choose to reach his Father or God. Jesus came here to empower us and teach us how to save ourselves through right thinking. He came here to assist souls; he did not come here to save Spirits, for our Spirits are perfect and eternal. Jesus came here to be an example and to show us how we can save ourselves. Each of us are responsible for our own salvation! Jesus did not come here to teach a religion or to take responsibility for all of humanity's sins. The highest way we can honor the life of Jesus is for us to live by his example. We need to activate our own Christ Consciousness and this can only occur when we choose to recognize the power within us and stop expecting someone *outside of ourselves*

13

to create the changes we desire to see. Jesus incarnated into a physical body to show us the way and to help us remember, "Ye are Gods". Each of us are extensions of God essence (we are one with God and each other) and it is only through ourselves that we can reach God. Jesus says, "The Father and I are One". All outer teachings such as this book, churches, teachers and organizations have the potential to lead you in the right direction and can be of great service and assistance. However, ultimately, it is only through remembering who you are, doing the inner work and choosing to reunite with your God self that will lead you to a true state of happiness bringing your own Heaven here down on Earth. Jesus clearly states, **"The Kingdom of God is within you!"** Outer teachings are important but it is the inner work and the integration of these outer teachings that will help you remember your perfection. See yourself and everyone else in their highest light, love yourself for all that you have ever been and most importantly: Remember who you are!

- Examine your life. What qualities and repetitive behaviors would you like to change?

- Make a list of everyone you have ever hurt. Talk to their Spirit, from the depths of your heart and apologize for any misqualified energy. Ask their Spirit to release you from any energetic entanglement that may have occurred. Ask your God self what lessons need to be learned so you won't repeat the pattern again.

- Make a list of anyone who has ever harmed you. Talk to their Spirit, from your heart, telling them exactly how you feel. Ask your God self what lessons need to be learned so you can move forward with true forgiveness.

- God experiences through us. Everything we choose to create is made with God's energy. Are your creations what you want God to be creating? Are your choices what you want God to be doing?

Insanity is when you keep doing the same thing and expect a different result.

Albert Einstein

My people are dying from lack of knowledge

Hosea 4:6

You cannot intellectualize your way to heaven. You can enter heaven only by absorbing my body and my blood, my living word and raising it to the whole loaf of your consciousness.

Matthew 13:3

Awareness of Thoughts

One of the most important steps in becoming a high vibrational being is becoming aware of your thoughts. Your mind is like a garden. Your thoughts (seeds) are what you plant and expect to grow. Constant awareness of your garden (mind) will help you create the reality you desire by helping you quickly pluck any weeds (negative thoughts) that have intruded upon your space. If your seeds are good thoughts, beliefs and ideas you will manifest a beautiful garden with a positive outcome. Begin now to sow thoughts of peace, happiness, healing, good will and abundance for yourself and the universe. Our world is held in place by our mind. Imagine how our world would be if each one of us were in control of our thoughts, beliefs and emotions 100% of the time. If we were all focused on unconditional love, peace and unity our world would reflect that. Just imagine!

All things are possible through the power of correct thought. Our thoughts and beliefs are "things". They are energy and energy never dies. When our energy or thoughts are focused and repetitive they become creative! When we realize our thoughts, feelings and beliefs create our reality we can create what we desire instead of being a victim of circumstances getting caught up in the after effects of our own negative thinking. The law of attraction simply states "like attracts like". Whatever we believe about others and ourselves becomes our reality. We literally see through our thoughts. Every thought we think is a lens we see through and it is the mind (our thoughts) that creates our feelings and emotions. As above in consciousness; so below in matter.

The vast majority of mankind currently lives in a world of unconscious co-creation. Many are running on autopilot and are unaware that their inner world (their thoughts, feelings and imagery) is where their creative power resides. Unfortunately, many of us are creating circumstances we don't really want because we are unaware that our thoughts, beliefs and subconscious programming is what creates our reality. Many of us have allowed our minds to get so out of control that our mind has literally become the enemy instead of the powerful gift of loving, co-creation God intended it to be. We each have the power to make our inner world work for us, or work against us. What we think about expands so any thought or belief that keeps us from our peace is a weed we want to discard from our garden immediately! The Universe fully supports us in every thought we choose to believe. It is a law of nature that the universe will reflect back to us what we are concentrating on. The Universe has no value judgments of positive or negative so we need to be very aware of where we are choosing to focus our attention!

We are each responsible for our own creations! We have the choice of being a conscious or unconscious co-creator with God. When we are making unconscious choices we are refusing to take command and dominion over our minds. When we become conscious we become aware and awareness is the key to change. We must be willing to put energy and time in avoiding negative thinking and actively pursuing to think positively. Persistent inner work and paying attention to what we are thinking will change our negative thought habits. If we are conscious of our thoughts, every negative thought can quickly be changed into a positive affirmation or command. If we are not happy with our life, we need to observe the attention of our thoughts and beliefs and shift our mindset into a more positive one.

We are created in God's image and likeness. We are created from God's energy; therefore, our energy is God's energy. We have the free will to apply God's energy any way we would like. Our attention is what directs that energy through our images, beliefs and feelings that we hold in our consciousness. Our focused energy accumulates and increases in intensity, so whatever we hold to be true in our thought system is what we will create for ourselves regardless if it is really true or not! There are no neutral thoughts. Every thought we think is either positive or negative, love or fear, God Self or ego, oneness or separation. It is believed that if we focus on something for 17 seconds, we activate the vibration and it becomes creative. Our thoughts literally create an energy frequency around us magnetizing those things we spend energy thinking about into a self-fulfilling prophecy. So we need to make sure we are focusing our energy in a positive direction so we can create what we want. Anything negative we have created in our reality, including all illness or dis-ease, comes from a thought or belief based in fear, separation, disempowerment and illusion. Decide now to break yourself free from the bondage of negative thinking. These creations are not the truth of your being. Your natural state of being is one of balance, unconditional love, unity, abundance, health, peace, joy and goodness. Decide not to be a victim of your thoughts! What you decide to focus on is your choice, so choose thoughts that are only focused on what you really want to create in your life! Choose love, choose peace, choose health, choose happiness! Your greatest power is your capacity to choose positive loving thoughts that are in alignment with your Spirit. When we create harmony and balance in our minds, we will find it in our lives.

- Keep a journal with you for one day and write down every negative thought you have. Later in the day, take each one of these negative thoughts and counteract it with a positive statement. The only way to change your negative thoughts is to become aware of them.
- What tapes are you playing in your head? If they aren't positive, delete them and record new ones. You must retrain your brain and move away from repetitive mind chatter.
- When you have a negative thought, immediately say, "dis-create" and restate what you do want.
- Recognize that all negative thoughts are out of alignment with the truth of your soul.
- You are an extension of God. Are your thoughts what you want God to be thinking?
- Are you a conscious creator of your life or do you allow others to create your life for you?
- Become a master of your mind and recognize when you are having obsessive thoughts. Immediately drop into your body, bring your full attention to what you are doing and shift your focus to your surroundings. Get out of your head and become fully immersed into the present moment. If your thoughts are obsessive you are in the past or the future…..pay attention!

Whether you believe you can or whether you believe you can't, you are right!
Henry Ford

It is the Mind that leads to the Christ.
Edgar Cayce

Most of us attract by default. We just think we don't have any control over it. Our thoughts and feelings are on autopilot, and so everything is brought to us by default.

Bob Doyle

As in heaven (your own mind), so on Earth (in your body and environment). This is the great law of life.

Dr. Joseph Murphy

The Universe is a big copy machine reproducing your thoughts in physical form that is your experience.

Neale Donald Walsh

Words are Powerful

Language is a powerful tool for directing and manifesting energy into form. We can change our lives in a matter of moments by changing our thoughts and the words we speak. Our words are powerful, so powerful that they create our reality. We are creating our future as we speak it! God created the Universe first through a thought and then with the spoken word, "Let there be Light". Our internal dialogue has an enormous effect on every aspect of our lives. Consider everything you think and say to be a prayer. Our words are powerful especially when we speak with very strong emotion. We literally speak things into being. Our words can be used to build or destroy, for light or dark purposes, to build someone up or tear them down. The words we speak and hear shape our lives. It is very important for us to become aware of how we are speaking. The universe always follows our command regardless if it is negative or positive. If you are struggling with negative thoughts and feelings, words and affirmations are a great way to reprogram yourself. We are very powerful creators and speaking things into being with strong emotion brings them into manifestation much quicker. In order to ensure the effectiveness of the affirmations focus your energy on your heart and repeat them with attention, conviction and strong desire.

Stating "I Am" before every statement is a very powerful command.

I AM a conscious Creator.

I AM one with God and all beings.

I AM one with the Light.

I AM a divine spark of God.

I AM beautiful.

I AM magnificent.

I AM eternal.

I AM full of courage.

I AM abundant.

I AM grateful.

I AM aware of my thoughts, words, feelings and emotions.

I AM a high vibrational being.

I AM made from love, therefore I AM love.

- Every morning before you get out of bed use words (with emotion) to affirm your intention for the day:

"My day flows with ease and grace"

"I Am grounded, balanced, kind, peaceful and joyful"

"I ask for my highest good to always be served."

"I exude peace, love, joy and compassion everywhere I go."

"All of my work is done with appreciation and gratitude"

"Infinite intelligence leads and guides me in all my ways"

- Become aware of your words. When you recognize you have stated something negative immediately say something positive to counteract your negative creation.

The word is a FORCE; it is the POWER you have to express and communicate, to think and thereby create the events in your life.

Don Miguel Ruiz

Life is a game of boomerangs. Our thoughts, deeds and words return to us sooner or later with astounding accuracy.

Florence Shinn

In the beginning was the word, and the word was with God and the word was God.

James 1:1

Words are alive, cut them and they bleed.

Ralph Waldo Emerson

Whatever words we utter should be chosen with care, for people will hear them and be influenced by them for good or evil.

Buddha

Death and life are in the power of the tongue.

Proverbs 18:21

Connecting to Our Feelings

Our feelings contain valuable information and connect us to our *intuition* and *truth*. **Feelings are the language of the soul!** When we suppress our feelings we suppress the guidance, wisdom and *connection* our soul wants to provide us. When we shut down our feelings, because we don't want to experience our pain, we create blocks and barriers between our physical and spiritual selves. This creates static interference within our being keeping us from accessing clear divine guidance that will help us to manifest the highest and best outcome in our lives. Our feelings also disclose lessons we need to learn and insights into our souls contract for this lifetime. Each feeling we experience is a repetition of many lifetimes of feelings that get brought to the surface for us to heal. When we disengage ourselves from our feelings we disconnect ourselves from our own internal guide and give our power away to others who like to make our decisions for us. We become powerless and do not trust our own intuition seeking all of our answers and guidance from outside sources. We become "thinkers" not "feelers". Thinking comes from the mind (ego) and always puts us in the past or in the future stripping us from our heart felt connection to the powerful, creative moment of the "Now". True power resides in the present moment. When we allow ourselves to *feel* our present moment feelings we can respond from our heart (soul) and not from our past wounds or our future concerns and worries. In order to raise our vibrations and access the truth of our being we will need to "feel" our way through this process not "think" our way through it.

We have been taught to avoid our feelings and resist allowing them to surface. Negative feelings left unaddressed get stuck in our energy body creating a foggy energy field that lowers our vibration and blocks our intuition. Unprocessed feelings become distortions that also lead to illness and dis-ease. When we ignore our feelings, because we don't want to feel the pain, we stuff them in our energy fields where they begin to fester. Eventually, our denied feelings move into the physical body and announce themselves as an imbalance, illness, pain, virus or disease. When we are connected to our feelings and allow ourselves to fully process through them, so we can release them, we become a clear vessel fully connected to the guidance of our soul and spirit. When we block, stuff or ignore our feelings our body will respond with a pain or symptom and let us know when we are out of alignment with our truth. Feelings are core sensations in the BODY; they are not created out of the MIND. Feelings are felt in the body and they are warning signs for us to acknowledge that something within our being needs to be addressed. The body never lies. It is always giving us warning signs…if we would only listen! We have a pill for every ailment: anxiety, high blood pressure, indigestion, depression even restless leg syndrome. We like to treat the symptom and avoid the root cause of the dis-ease while the body continuously tries to get our attention prompting us to recognize that something within our being needs to be addressed. As Deepak Chopra says, *"Divine Intelligence is the spark of life that animates every living cell in the body."* Our body is a field of divine intelligence, energy and divine organization. It is in a constant state of regeneration, therefore, any discomfort whether it be emotional, mental or physical is a sign that our soul is out of alignment with its spiritual self.

Our feelings simply want to be felt and when we step into allowance and allow our feelings to be felt, without placing judgment on them, we can access vital information that can help us shift unhealthy beliefs, recognize repetitive behavioral patterns, make better choices and heal our bodies. All we really need to do is allow and honor the process. **When we allow ourselves to pause at our feelings, instead of ignoring them or leaping forward into our emotions, we put ourselves in a place of power.** When we become aware of our feelings we can retrieve the information they are trying to provide us and respond from a place of spiritual understanding instead of reactive ego-based thinking. Unfortunately, humanity as a whole, has chosen to suppress their feelings literally closing down their hearts due to years of stored pain. This causes us to become numb – unable to feel or experience our feelings - leading us to react from a place of fear, disconnection, confusion and powerlessness. We fall into the illusion of victim hood believing we are victims of circumstances. Unfortunately, this way of "thinking" and not "feeling" keeps us running on autopilot totally disconnected from our higher wisdom where we will continue to draw negative situations to us that evoke the very feelings - stored within our being - that need to be looked at, felt and *released*.

Remember, we are energetic and physical beings. Our energetic body is very similar to the layers of an onion. When we allow ourselves to feel an old wound or childhood trauma we have stuffed in our energy field the wound will open and we will experience the pain once again. However, it is rising through the many layers of the energy body to be released. Depending on the severity of the trauma, the feeling may need to be experienced several times before it finally rises to the surface for final releasement and healing. All of our stored negative emotions, feelings and past traumas are toxic matter that must be moved out of our energetic bodies before true healing and a merging with our God self can occur. Oftentimes we get stuck in our story, resist our feelings and emotions and choose not to do the inner work because it can be a painful process. However, true healing is spiritual healing (the healing of the soul) and all lower vibrating toxic debris must be brought to the surface to be released. Allow yourself to feel, so you can heal your wounded feelings. We must process through them, resolve them and release them so we can clear out our emotional body creating a clear vehicle for our soul. If we resist a feeling we hold it to us and it continues to persist. If anger arises, feel it fully, so your anger does not turn into a reactive emotion. Once your anger is felt, you will release it and there will be no need to react in an angry way to every person or situation you interact with for the rest of your day. If someone makes you angry, allow yourself "private" time to go into your anger. Ask your anger questions and retrieve the message it is trying to bring you. Allow yourself to fully feel it, instead of resisting it, so you can set yourself free. After you have felt your anger, you will be able to rationally approach the other person from a non-reactive place. You will be able to speak to them from a place of honesty and integrity shedding light on the situation so it can be resolved and not repeated again in the future. Emotions, feelings, thoughts and beliefs are real things. They are living energy forms naked to the average eye but can be seen by people who are clairvoyant. Just because the majority of humanity cannot see these energy forms does not mean they are not there. What we resist continues to persist in our energetic being and we will continue to magnetize situations into our life that will force us to address all of our unresolved, stored, hidden feelings.

Once we allow our feelings to rise to the surface to be felt and fully experienced, we can then use our awareness to consciously shift our feelings one vibration, one frequency, one thought and one emotion at a time. It is our responsibility to become aware of our feelings and to recognize that our feelings do affect the whole of humanity. When we become aware of our feelings and fully allow ourselves to experience them, we will dissolve them freeing up areas in our energy body so we can hold more light and a higher vibration. Our higher vibrating energy affects others so not only are we healing ourselves, we are also inspiring others to heal simply by allowing ourselves to raise our vibration. When we are vibrating in the pure high frequencies of joy, gratitude and appreciation we are fully open to our own source of intuitive divine guidance. When we shut down our feelings we also shut down our intuitive guidance because Spirit communicates to us through our feelings. Our feelings are how we tap into our intuition and truth. Without feelings, we have no internal guide.

- We are each responsible for releasing our own feelings. If we are disconnected from our feelings we will not be able to fully feel, heal and release them. They will get stored in our emotional field and we will end up projecting all of our unprocessed feelings and emotions onto everyone else blaming them for the conditions in our lives. The next time a feeling arises, allow yourself to go as deep into it as you can. Ask yourself, "What am I feeling right now? Is it fear, sadness, helplessness, abandonment, rejection?" Is the feeling I am feeling right now really a present moment feeling or is this a feeling I have not healed from my past? Identify it and allow yourself to fully move through it so it can be released and not projected onto everyone else you come into contact with.

- If we resist a feeling we keep it and it continues to persist. If we allow ourselves to feel it fully, we will let go of it. If anger arises, feel it. Feeling it doesn't mean expressing anger to someone else….then it becomes an emotion, a reaction. Simply recognize that you are feeling angry. Allow yourself to fully feel your anger and ask your anger what it has to teach you. Continue to feel it until it is gone.

- Examine your life. What feelings have been redundant? What situations do you continue to draw to yourself that evoke a feeling in you that has been stored in your energy field and needs to be looked at so it can be demagnetized and released?

- How do you feel about yourself? How do you feel about others? Do you see them as an extension of yourself making different choices or do you see them as separate?

- As a child were you allowed to express your feelings and emotions in a healthy way?

- What are your most predominant feelings?

Whatever we are thinking, feeling, saying, or doing, we are co-creating, empowering and magnetizing into our lives.

Patricia Cota Robles

The pain of all our hurts may be quite intense, but it also softens us and completes itself in the process of being felt.

Susan Thesenga

If you allow all the negative thoughts to come forth into consciousness and the negative feelings to flow with the positive intent to heal yourself, then you will not get stuck in negativity that will harm you. Express the negative feelings with the intention to release them, let them go, and move on beyond them. This will help heal you and you will not get sick.

Barbara Brennan

Normality is the capacity to express your feelings. From the moment that you don't fear to share your heart, you are a free person.

Paulo Coelho

Emotional Clearing

We experience feelings yet we generate emotions. Feelings are passive; emotions are reactive. E-motions are "energy in motion." Feelings are not created from the mind; they are core sensations in the body such as heartache from a wounded heart or nausea from sadness or grief. Emotions are feelings with a thought attached. As soon as we feel a feeling and allow the negative mind chatter to take over we have activated our emotions. Feelings and emotions usually go hand and hand and they simply want to be acknowledged, felt and expressed. All feelings and emotions that are fully experienced, *in a healthy way*, acknowledged for the information they are trying to provide and are fully released from our system will create more space within our being for our divine spirit to flow through us bringing greater peace into our lives.

Emotions are one of the most beautiful parts of a human being and they should not be denied, suppressed or judged. Many of us have given a great deal of our energy and power away to our emotions because we have not allowed ourselves to fully express them. We end up holding onto them for years giving them great power to control us. When we allow them to be expressed we allow them the freedom to be released. If we deny our emotions we end up fragmenting ourselves creating all kinds of alter egos that get stored in our energy body. We need to experience our emotions so we can understand them. Unfortunately, we have been taught to resist our emotions and to quickly disconnect and stuff them leading many of us to completely shut down our emotional body. As a child, we were told not to cry, not to raise our voice, don't talk back, don't get mad, be nice and be quiet. Although our parents meant well, it was very damaging to us as Spirits because we ended up storing all of our emotions in our energy body and we became very reactive, explosive, emotionally unbalanced adults. Many of us do not understand or know how to properly express our emotions in a healthy way. Drama, blame and over reactivity have become the norm, which always throws us out of alignment with our higher wisdom. When we are triggered by a situation each of us must learn to stand in our power, speak our truth from a place of integrity and ground our light. Choose not to react to the person in an unbalanced way. If you feel your emotional body taking over, simply walk away but make sure you process through your emotions and feelings later. When you have calmed down, observe the situation from a higher perspective. Ask yourself how are you feeling, what is your body saying to you? Where are you holding discomfort in your body? Where are your thoughts? Do you have thoughts and emotions that need to be addressed? Ask your thoughts, feelings and emotions questions. What are they trying to say to you? Avoid being reactive but address your pain. Negative feelings and emotions need to be released before we will truly be able to love and have compassion for ourselves and everyone else.

Our emotional health is what determines our state of being. Due to emotional distress, most of us have disconnected from our feeling self and pushed our negative emotions deep into the recesses of our being. In order to release our pain and achieve balance and good health it is necessary for us to bring our emotions to the surface so they can be fully experienced and felt. Denying how we feel brings self-destruction and disease within our system. Unexpressed and repressed emotions must come out. They will find a way of showing themselves so it is in our best interest to go ahead and deal with them when they arise so they don't explode on others at inappropriate times. Angry explosions, yelling and crying for no reason, mood swings, depression, anxiety, stress, body aches and illness all have messages they are trying to reveal to us, if we would only listen. Past memories, emotional trauma and feelings need to be addressed, acknowledged and integrated before we can heal and bring ourselves into wholeness. If we are to fully awaken and ground our God self into our being we will need to liberate ourselves from the entanglement of our past. Full attention, acceptance, allowance and forgiveness are the most powerful ways for us to deal with our repressed emotions.

Transformation can only occur when we choose to process through our feelings and emotions. Blame, anger, resentment and hatred are sure-fire indicators that our emotions have not been fully integrated and released. Toxic emotions will only hurt us, not the people we are upset with. By harboring these intense feelings we will continue to attract people into our life who also have the same emotional problems and each of us will feed off of each others negative emotional energy. Like energy attracts like energy and our souls will continue to bring people to us who will reflect back to us our own inner state of emotional instability. When we decide to transmute our lower vibrational emotions we will no longer attract lower vibrating relationships into our life. We need to give ourselves permission to feel and express everything within our being. Once we have allowed ourselves to release a lot of our emotional blocks we will become less reactive and will be able to stay grounded and hold our center when we encounter a difficult situation or soul lesson. This will allow ourselves to bypass our emotional mode and step into the observer mode where we can determine the stimulus that kicks off our emotional responses so we can neutralize them. Usually, our knee jerk reactions are shining light on a childhood core belief or fear that is not based in truth. Our feelings and emotions are important and they are valid! We need to learn how to honor them so we can process through the pain but gain the wisdom our emotions are trying to give us.

As the Earth rises in vibration we are being forced to look at and heal our stuffed negative emotions and feelings. Being passive, complacent and in denial about our emotions and feelings will keep us stuck in the lower vibrations of duality. We must strive to become emotionally mature, truthful and conscious with ourselves about our inner workings / inner psychology so we can become a grounded and fully empowered being. Many people speak the right words, but inside their emotional body is a whole different reality. We may be able to mask or disguise our emotions, temporarily, but that does not mean they have disappeared. Whatever we are carrying within our emotional body is what we are creating in our lives. If we don't learn how to acknowledge, feel and release our emotions, our emotions will run us.

The current chaos in our world is a reflection of our inner chaos. We will never have peace in this world until we have peace within ourselves. Our society has avoided truly connecting with their feelings and emotions for thousands of years. All emotional events that we have not dealt with are like magnetic images stuck in our energy field. Every time they get activated we have the opportunity to de-magnetize these stuck images if we allow ourselves to fully feel our emotions when they arise. Unfortunately, most of us resist this process and we become reactive responding from a place of pain instead of a place of love and compassion. We are stuffers and our baggage is full! We have done everything we can to avoid experiencing our pain. We take drugs, overindulge in alcohol and food, submerse ourselves in our work, become shopaholics, continually seek out doctors for pharmaceuticals and get fixated on other peoples problems in order to avoid our own. We project all of our "stuff" onto everyone else never taking responsibility for our own inner issues that need to be healed. As long as we are in denial of our negative emotions and feelings we will never be able to transmute and release them. The energy we have created for ourselves within our own energy field cannot be destroyed. Energy never dies! It stays with us until we decide to transform it into a higher vibrational energy. Many of us are in denial of our toxic energy and are psychologically lazy. However, the additional light flooding this planet is shaking up our emotional bodies and bringing our stuff to the surface to be healed and released. It is time to lighten our load!

- Take the time to reconnect with three events in your past where you were not able to truly express how you felt. Write a letter to yourself, the people involved or to the circumstance allowing yourself to get in touch with those suppressed feelings. Then burn it, rip it up or bury it setting your intention to release all toxic emotions.

- Re-examine your week. Where have you allowed yourself to stuff your emotions? Have you been dishonest with yourself in order to avoid hurting someone else's feelings at the expense of your own?

- Where have you emotionally "over reacted" in the past year? Are you accustomed to not speaking your truth about how you really feel eventually allowing things to explode to such a point you have no control over your emotions?

- Set your intention to become aware of your emotions and feelings. When something arises and you are not able to compassionately express it to the other person involved, make the commitment to yourself to express it in privacy. Your emotions are important and they are valid. If you resist them they will persist. They will get stored in your energy body just waiting for the next opportunity for them to be released.

- Do not fear your emotions. Befriend them. When they arise ask them questions. Notice how you feel and ask them why they are here. Ask them what they have to teach you.

- We should not take our emotions out onto other people. If we are not careful, our emotions can create additional karma for us. We need to learn how to balance, express and release them in a **positive way**. Because they are reactive, they can affect our health, if we do not learn to deal with them through constructive means. It is best to feel our feelings, but control our emotions and reactive behaviors.

1. Go to your room, shut the door and scream! Screaming is a great way to release pent up energies. Set your intention to release everything that no longer serves you and scream into a pillow with all of your being.

2. Allow yourself to cry. Tears enable us to get in touch with our deepest feelings. Weeping arises from the heart and is a gift of grace from God.

3. Emotional wounds are stored in the tissues of the body and in your energy fields that surround your body. Exercise is a great way to move stuck energy. Yoga, walking, running, rebounding, dancing etc….helps keep your energy flowing and assists in removing emotional blocks held within the body.

4. Find a great energy healer! Energy work will greatly assist you in moving out stuck energy that is ready to be released. There are many modalities to choose from. Pick one you resonate with: DNA Theta Healing, Reiki, Tai Chi, Cranial Sacral, EMC2, EMF Balancing, Rosen Method, Polarity Therapy, Rolfing, Acupuncture.

Emotions can work for you or against you. You can choose how they will affect you.

Adam, Dream Healer

The mind is a movie projector. It places images on the screen called our world. Change the projector and you will change the movie on the screen.

Gary Renard

Turn your wounds into wisdom.

Oprah Winfrey

The will to live is emotional. It is an emotion so deep that we could call it an innate yearning to exist in a state of beingness.

Barbara Dewey

Tears are words the heart can't express.

Unknown

Our souls return to us as we reclaim all our feelings. Our anger, fear and grief can turn into joy and exhilaration if we let all our emotions flow.
Susan Thesenga

Accepting Responsibility

You are an extension of God, a co-creator and it is YOU (the totality of your being both conscious and unconscious) who draws all experiences to yourself in order to heal and advance your soul. Until you own your creations, you will not be able to change them. We are powerless to change anything when we are in our victim consciousness. When we can say to ourselves, "I accept responsibility for everything I have created in my life" we are in a place of power fully able to take control over our life circumstances.

Nothing in our lives can happen to us unless our soul is in agreement to experience it. There are no victims, each of us are responsible for our own creations. Before we incarnate we go through a process of pre-birth planning. We choose our parents, our sexual identity, where we want to live and the lessons and circumstances we want to master. Our lessons are chosen by us and they are reflective of past life issues we had problems with, karma that needs to be resolved and agreements we set up with other souls in order to assist each of us with our soul lessons. Those who have hurt us the most are the very ones we have shared many lives with and are the ones who love us the most. They are our soul mates and usually there are lessons for each person involved. Once we incarnate, everyone on a human level forgets what we signed up for because if we remembered, we would not be able to act out our parts in order for us to balance our karma and learn our lessons. We incarnate on Earth under the veil of forgetfulness with preset mental, emotional, physical and spiritual challenges. Our most difficult lessons to overcome reap the greatest benefits and are the quickest way for us to learn from our preset goals and life challenges. In order for us to learn a lesson about forgiveness someone has to do something to us in order for us to forgive. If our lesson is to learn how to manage anger in a healthy way then someone needs to make us angry in order for us to learn how to express our anger *without denying it* or exploding in an irrational way.

Karma that needs to be resolved is neutral and a form of learning, it is not judgment or punishment. It simply seeks energetic balance. Karma is not created with another individual. Once you create karma it is YOUR karma. If you have created a situation with another being that creates pain, it is your responsibility to address it immediately. Otherwise, you will hold a negative energetic imprint within your energy field and through the Universal Law of Attraction, you will attract another situation to create balance within your being regardless if it is with the same person or not. The key here is to learn from our miscreations and misqualified energy so we can clear our energy field of any energetic imprints or magnets that continue to magnetize repetitive negative circumstances into our life.

Every person that comes into our life, on a soul level, has agreed to play a role for us in order to help us advance our spiritual growth. Many people refer to us as being actors in a play, students in Earth school, or players in a game making choices that move us closer or further away from God. Obviously, greater advancement is made when we make choices that are in alignment with our God self and not from our lower self or ego. When we view our lives from a higher perspective we can see that all crisis and trials are opportunities for spiritual and personal growth. Every difficult interaction is a spiritual test leading us into self-mastery and wholeness. Everything has value and because we do not remember our contracted lessons or know the life blueprint of other souls we need to be very careful about passing judgment on each other's learning experiences. Once our lessons are learned, the energy is balanced and there is no need to keep repeating the same old lessons. Any judgment on our part creates additional karma and that is the last thing we want to do.

Our contracted relationships are a catalyst for transformation and are our greatest tool for awakening. Our spiritual selves, residing in a higher dimension, are always in communication with each other making agreements and setting up situations to help everyone heal and master their soul lessons. We have free will and can choose to respond to these situations in a negative or positive way. Once our lessons are learned, karma is balanced and we transcend our lower selves we will graduate and move into the final dimension of God. When this occurs, we will no longer need to incarnate into a physical vehicle to learn difficult soul lessons. Once we awaken to this concept and realize that every difficult situation we have drawn to ourselves is an opportunity to advance our soul, we will consciously and actively start playing the game to our advantage. We will begin to recognize all the key players or soul mates in our life and begin to see that each one of them has actually gifted us with a learning opportunity, even though it may have been through a difficult soul lesson.

Currently, Earth is moving out of the cyclic period of darkness and into the golden age of en-lighten-ment where learning through karma will no longer be necessary. Because of this, each of us are balancing and transforming our misqualified energy or karma and healing our lower selves at an ***accelerated rate***. It is divine plan and we cannot fully pass through the photon belt and into the higher frequencies until we have released our unbalanced energy or extra baggage from our current and previous lifetimes. Each of us are going through a massive clearing and our God self is bringing very intense lessons to us to learn from. Our God self is not punishing us and we should not fear these circumstances when they arise. However, if we remain alert and in the present moment, we can become observers of the situation enabling us to be less reactive and more in control. When we accept responsibility and recognize that we are in a spiritual lesson we can quickly take dominion over our lower selves moving through the situation with ease and grace helping us to release all the energetic patterns and karmic miasims that are ready to be released.

Emotional baggage, distorted subconscious programs and karma are cleared one layer at a time with each issue consisting of many layers. Every time we clear a layer we release our blocks and get closer and closer to merging with our God self. The majority of our layers are from past lives brought into this lifetime for healing. If the layers aren't cleared our God self will create additional circumstances with additional people to help us finally learn our lessons and clear out our misqualified energy. Our Spiritual self or God self loves us unconditionally and never judges us if we make a mistake. Mistakes are part of the human experience, however, our God self wants us to clear our blocks and raise our vibration so it can merge with our soul and physical being bringing our Spirit down into matter. We do not have to be perfect in order to clear our blocks, we simply need to be making progress and be pro-active in our efforts doing the best we can to learn our lessons even if that means a lesson is learned through our mistakes. The spiritual path is filled with detours, illusions, ups and downs, challenges and temptations that will take us off our path. The expansion of our consciousness, healing and growth takes time and can be very subtle or very abrupt. All that is needed from us is the courage, intention and willingness to transcend ourselves moving beyond our current level of consciousness into a higher level of consciousness helping us to remember who we are bringing the truth of our being (our divine spiritual essence) down into the Earth plane.

Unfortunately, many of us have been stuck in the wheel of reincarnation because we have not listened to our God self's guidance and we forgot who we were. Our free will is honored and our God self will not tell us what to do. However, if we choose to ASK and LISTEN our God self will give us greater understanding and guide us in the right direction by helping us to transcend our current level of being into a more expanded one. It is easy for us to get caught up in the illusion of our physical reality forgetting we have a direct connection to our own source of higher wisdom and divine guidance. When we allow ourselves to be absorbed by the dramas and physicality of Earth life we end up creating additional karma for ourselves by blocking out our inner source of truth and wisdom allowing our egos to make decisions for us. Our egos lead us in the wrong direction by getting us to focus on external belief systems, wealth and ego accomplishments rather than the growth and expansion of our inner spirit. Where we place our attention is precious, whatever we focus on expands. Many of us have acquired great material wealth and accumulated a lot of physical things at the expense of lowering our vibration through our feelings of anger, greed, stress, jealousy and competition creating blocks and barriers to our spiritual self. We blocked ourselves from our own divine guidance and started looking for guidance and God in physical things and places. We forgot our divinity while money and ego gratification became our new source of fulfillment. Unfortunately, fulfillment through physicality is empty and illusory. Connection with our eternal God self is far more important and is the only true source of nourishment, security and happiness.

The greatest gift God has given us is the freedom of free will choice. We each have the choice to create our lives from a place of fear or a place of love. Unfortunately, many of us are making choices from a place of fear. We live in fear of never having enough or being enough and we live in fear of hurting someone else's feelings or being wrong. We allow other peoples opinions, beliefs and truths to become our own. We chose to give our power away and we have lost touch with the essence of our true being disconnecting our selves from our own intuitive inner guide. We have become like sheep in a flock following the herd, even though the herd is headed straight off the cliff. The question you must ask yourself now is, "Do I want a safe life that meets expected conformity or do I want an authentic life?" In order to live from our own truth we must take the time to examine our lives, accept personal responsibility for our choices and become pro-active when we notice we are out of alignment with our God self. We must go beyond the norm and believe in ourselves and not get caught in our own self imposed personal stagnation because we are allowing others to make decisions for us. We must take personal responsibility for everything that has occurred and will occur in our life. From this moment forward we need to declare our sovereignty as a divine being. We are God in action and we are the masters of our own life. We need to start making empowered choices from our heart, not our mind and we will always be guided in the right direction. Each of us needs to accept responsibility for the condition of our lives and become masterful at creating what we want. Everything that happens to us is there for our own soul's growth. There are lessons to be learned and a deeper meaning to be discovered in even the most troublesome events. We must accept responsibility for everything that occurs to us and stop avoiding the changes we need to make in order to evolve into our highest soul's potential.

In order to do this we need to bring into our awareness the many ways in which we create our current life circumstances:

1. Pre-birth Contracts or Soul Charts are created with our soul mates to help each of us balance our karma and learn specific lessons that need to be mastered. Remember, karma is not punishment! When our karma presents itself, acknowledge it for what it is….misqualified energy from our past seeking balance in our present day situation. This is an opportunity for healing and the quicker we can step out of resistance and move into gratitude for the opportunity to create balance within our soul the easier this process will be.

2. Unconscious emotions, feelings, thoughts, distorted beliefs and behavioral patterns that are stored in our subconscious mind. Both our ego and our shadow thrive on these repressed and rejected aspects of our being. If we continue to deny they exist these "fragmented sub personalities" will continue to bring unwanted experiences into our life forcing us to acknowledge, accept and heal them.

3. Free will: Everything in our life is not predetermined! Although our soul contracts must be honored, we also have free will and the power of choice to choose how quickly we would like to evolve. We have the free will choice to follow our ego's guidance keeping us stuck in repetitive circumstances or we can follow the guidance of our God self and learn our lessons moving into self mastery.

4. Law of Attraction: "Like Attracts Like" Whatever we are thinking, feeling, speaking, believing, doing and being sends out a vibration attracting like energy to us. If we are choosing to participate in high vibrational activities we will attract high vibrational situations into our life. Likewise, if we are focused on negativity, judgment, fear, lack, separation, addiction, chaos and drama that is exactly what we will draw into our lives to experience.

- Examine your life. Determine who your soul mates are and what lessons they have come here to teach you. What lessons have you signed up to teach others?

- Are you making *truly* free choices or are you allowing those choices to be made for you? Your free will is your divine birthright. Many of us have given up our "right to choose" by allowing our unconscious mind, ego and "others" to inadvertently create our beliefs and life situations for us. We unconsciously gave up our free will. Become conscious about your choices and take back your power by tapping into your own divine intelligence system.

- Are you choosing to participate in high vibrational activities or low vibrational activities? Where are you choosing to invest your energy? Bring everything you do into your conscious awareness. Resist being on autopilot and become the master of your energy.

Your personal consciousness is entirely responsible for whatever comes into your life and personal experience. It is your personal consciousness which brings you good or evil.

Christ Letters from Christ Way

Man must cease attributing his problems to his environment and learn again to exercise his will - his personal responsibility.

Albert Schweitzer

When we have begun to take charge of our lives, to own ourselves, there is no longer any need to ask permission of someone.

George O'neil

Understanding Mirrors

You are the creator of your life and you must accept responsibility for all of your creations. All that you create for yourself is you loving you even when you have created a difficult situation. Your creation is for the purpose of greater awareness, understanding, healing, energetic balance and soul advancement. If you are in denial of the crappy stuff in your life you are rejecting your creatorship and have chosen to be powerless. God gave you free will and you have the power to change. In order to change your reality, you must first accept it as part of your own creation.

Each of us must accept responsibility and realize that the only problems in our life stems from our own unconscious behaviors and free will choices. God does not create suffering; *humans* create suffering! Through attention, self-examination, reflection, conscious awareness of our core beliefs, emotions and feelings we will be able to heal and release the majority of our life problems. Everything always goes back to SELF. Fortunately, the universe is on our side providing us with a mirror so we can see ourselves. If we are seeing something in someone else we don't like, it is also within us. Likewise, if there is something we don't like within our being we will see it in everyone else. Our outer reality is a mirror of our inner being. Everything we see in our family or in another human being is a reflection of our own inner being. We would not be able to recognize their imperfections unless they were within us as well. Likewise, if we admire someone and find qualities within them we really like we must understand that those qualities are also within us.

Our God self is always bringing people and situations into our life to show us things within ourselves that need to be healed. The universe is our mirror and until we heal the distortions contained within our energy fields we will continue to run into ourselves everywhere we go. We attract relationships with certain individuals so they can show us areas in our own life that need to be healed through their actions and behaviors. These contracts are formed because both people are working on the same core beliefs that need to be seen, acknowledged and released. The other person acts as our mirror so we can see ourselves. Everyone reflects back to us the relationship we are having with ourselves. They are there to shed light on an aspect of ourselves that needs healing. Denial and suppression keeps us in the cycle of recreation until we learn the lessons they are here to teach. We cannot be an empowered and enlightened being and also see ourselves as a victim of circumstances. No one is a victim. Everything is created for you by you in perfect design. Nothing in the Universe is by chance, everything is carefully designed for each soul's unique growth. It is now time for each of us to remember who we are and to actively participate with our spiritual self in learning our lessons and clearing out our energetic bodies. Our personal vibration rises as we master our soul lessons eventually bringing us into divine alignment with our God self. Once this occurs we will no longer need to continue to draw negative lower vibrational circumstances or people into our lives.

- When you find yourself in a negative situation ask yourself: "What is this person reflecting back to me?" What behavior, thought or belief does this person have that I also need to heal within my own being?

- There are usually 3 reasons for a mirror:
  1. Someone is being a mirror for you to show you how you are thinking, feeling, behaving, vibrating. They are a reflection of a lesson you need to learn. Usually both people have the same core belief or issue that needs to be healed. Both are reflections for each other. This is the mirror most commonly used!
  2. You have volunteered on a soul level to be a mirror for someone else. Through their actions, words, beliefs etc.….you have chosen to hold the space for them so they could behave or react out of alignment and "see" and "feel" the pain they have inflicted on you. **IF** they witness your pain and "acknowledge" their behavior they will be less likely to repeat the lesson again and will clear their karma. Through experience and consequences lessons are learned **IF** the person is willing to accept responsibility transcending the need to repeat the lesson in the future.
  3. If you have done a lot of work on yourself, another person can reflect your progress. People will reflect back to you lessons you have recently moved through. They are seeking assistance from you to help shed light on the situation so they can also move forward without having to repeat the same lesson over and over. In this case, you provide a new perspective and are a lighthouse lighting the way for others helping them to bring their unconsciousness forward into the light of awareness so it can be healed.

- Understand that mirrors are not about the "story". The mirror is about the feelings and reactions the "story" provokes within us. Do not get hung up on the He said/ She said, "story". Focus on the interaction and how it made you **feel** and how you wanted to react. The reflection is about the feeling that needs to be transformed within yourself. If there is no feeling or need to react there is nothing you need to transform. Look for the emotion!

- If someone is mistreating you, ask yourself: " How am I mistreating my soul or the soul of someone else? Where am I being abusive?

- Become your own Inner Witness and ask yourself:

1. What is this person or circumstance trying to teach me?
2. What behavior are they revealing that is a mirror of my behavior?
3. What negative thoughts and beliefs am I holding onto that need to be released?
4. What am I allowing to be drawn to me? Have I been negative or positive lately? Where am I holding my vibration?
5. Am I evolving or revolving? Where am I repeating the same things over and over? What is the pattern?
6. What is the gift (lesson) they are trying to give to me?
7. What is the gift (lesson) I am trying to give to another?

Life is a mirror and will reflect back to the thinker what he thinks into it. Ernest Holmes

There are two ways of spreading light; to be the candle or the mirror that reflects it. Edith Wharton

The secret of life is that God has created a universe that acts like a mirror. You are living in your own personal house of mirrors. You are literally the center of your own personal universe. If you want your outer situation to change you must begin by changing your inner situation because the Universe can only reflect back to you what you send out. If you want the universal mirror to show you a smiling face, you must first smile at the universe.

Kim Michaels

Mastering Soul Lessons

Families are our greatest indicators of where the bulk of our soul lessons reside. Our past is a huge part of our story. In order to learn from our soul lessons and create a new story we must embrace the past without avoiding it, denying it, placing judgment or blame on it. Our soul and God self carefully chose the family line that would give us the greatest opportunity for soul growth. Our families show us the very things we need to own, heal and learn from. If these lessons aren't learned, families find themselves revolving in a vicious cycle of disharmony. It takes great strength and perseverance for a soul to pull themselves out of this chaotic, toxic energy so they can view the situation from a higher perspective, learn the lessons and begin to heal. This type of chaos can also be a catalyst to move a soul forward into transformation. Tremendous soul advancement is made when a being is able to move into their feelings, emotions and pain from their family history and strive to release all blame, resentment, anger and hatred.

Once our soul lessons are learned and we choose to heal and move into a place of unconditional love, forgiveness and compassion our vibrations will begin to rise rapidly. As we rise in vibration ALL of our relationships will change because we are changing. Some of our relationships will rise in vibration with us and some relationships we may have to let go of. This can be one of the most empowering and freeing things we can do for ourselves, as well as, one of the most difficult. It is not healthy for anyone to artificially sustain an unhealthy relationship. Once we raise our vibrations, we will naturally want to surround ourselves with relationships that are based in the new energy of love, compassion, joy, acceptance and peace. Lower vibrating relationships cannot be brought up into a new space of higher vibrating energy unless each person is willing to accept responsibility for their own healing. Unfortunately, many people will resist this process because they will have to connect with their heart, their feeling center. This can be a very difficult task because we oftentimes avoid acknowledging our true feelings and emotions, keeping ourselves in denial, which will block us from accessing the higher vibrations. Many souls are not ready for a breakthrough and are not ready to release the pain and suffering in their hearts. They will choose to hold onto their pain because they live in fear of accessing those parts of themselves they have disowned and rejected for so long.

The level of desire and the willingness to change and look within ourselves will determine how quickly we shift, master our lessons and raise our vibration. Intention is everything. Some of our soul mates will choose to continue to experience the lower vibrating energy of fear and disconnection. Stepping into a state of allowance and staying detached from the situation will be necessary. Unconditional love is allowing our soul mates the freedom to choose whether they want to shift their vibration or not. Many will cling to their old ways and will not choose to shift their frequency. It will be difficult to maintain relationships with people who choose to stay stuck in the old energy while you are focused on transcending it. Some of your soul mates may not know how to respond to you when you begin to respond to them in a new way. They may try to push your buttons and keep you from moving forward. Have great compassion for them but understand that you no longer have to participate in their soul lessons. Your soul mates will draw another being into their circle for them to continue to learn from and gain greater soul growth and clarity. Be supportive but stay detached. Sometimes people will have to experience the same lesson over and over again until they finally learn from it. This can be a painful process. Part of your new lesson may be to learn how to stand in your power, how to use discernment and how to be unconditionally loving without allowing yourself to get sucked into someone else's drama. Eventually, everyone who chooses will rise in vibration. It is divine plan. Make the conscious choice right now to attract relationships that empower and enhance your light and vibration. There is no need for you to sacrifice your happiness, joy and energy for someone else's. No one needs to sacrifice anything. The universe is abundant with love, joy, compassion and peace. Every person has a choice as to what they want to experience - a life based on love or a life based on fear.

In order for us to move forward with our journey into healing and wholeness, we may need to release relationships that are holding us back from reaching our highest soul's potential. Each of us will know in our hearts which relationships have had their time. Set your intention to learn the lessons these people have reflected to you and love yourself enough to give yourself the space you need to bring yourself back into alignment with your highest good. Sometimes it takes our soul mates longer to learn their lessons. If we cannot heal these relationships, lovingly release them holding each individual in their highest light while you continue to evolve. Everyone is on a different consciousness level and we do not learn our lessons at the same time. The healing work we do on ourselves will affect our soul mates and the rest of humanity energetically, so it is possible that these relationships in the future may be healed. Stay focused on your healing knowing that the relationships that are meant to be a part of your life will be there effortlessly, naturally and lovingly.

- Locate 3 childhood events that repeated themselves later in your life. What were the events trying to teach you?
- Examine your parents, siblings and grandparents. Whatever negative traits you see within them are also within you and can only be recognized if YOU need to work on them as well. What traits have been passed down generation to generation?

- What negative traits within your family have you overcome? Are you a better parent? Have you overcome addictions? Are you aware of your creatorship and consciously creating a positive life for yourself? Are you compassionate? Are you actively working on forgiveness? Do you see the divinity in all beings? Are you aware of your thoughts, feelings and beliefs?
- What are you going to do with your soul lessons? Are you going to use your soul lessons as a platform for victimization or for empowerment and soul growth?

The way you will experience and feel about yourself is not determined by how other people look and feel about you. The way that you will experience and feel about yourself is actually determined by how YOU look at and think about THEM. Whatever we think about others is really like sending a message about ourselves to our self.

Gary Renard

We say we exchange words when we meet. What we exchange is souls.

Minot Savage

You do not face difficulties as punishment; you attract them because you are moving to the next level of understanding your sacred nature.

Sonia Choquette

Are you going to work from your back bone or your wish bone?

Leonard Crohn

The design of your life…the people, places and events in it have all been perfectly created for you by you.

Neale Donald Walsh

Forgiveness

When we fully accept responsibility for our lives knowing that we are the creator of our entire life experience and remember that we are not powerless victim of circumstances, how could we not forgive those who have harmed us? Forgiveness has nothing to do with the other person; it has everything to do with you, your own inner freedom and desire to move forward in your life. Each life experience has made you the person you are today and it is your soul who has chosen to experience these circumstances. Nothing can happen to you unless your soul is in agreement to experience those life challenges for your own soul's growth. Your soul chose your life circumstances in order to best serve your continuing evolution.

Forgiveness is not a thought, an idea or a mental concept. True forgiveness is a process of greater understanding and analysis. It requires attention, healing and time…. it does not occur instantaneously. In order to truly forgive, each of us must process through the full range of lessons, feelings and emotions associated with the traumatic events in our lives. Blind forgiveness is the easy way out and is usually the route most people prefer. Blind forgiveness is denial and avoidance. It helps people brush things under the rug without ever getting to the root cause of the problem. Unfortunately, this leads to a pattern of recreation in the future because it was never properly addressed. You cannot change a problem with the same state of consciousness that created the problem.

In addition, blind forgiveness is a way for people to avoid truly getting in touch with their feelings. When we avoid our feelings we hold onto them, stuffing them in our energy fields giving them great power. These stuffed feelings become reactive emotions fueling the fires of emotional imbalance, depression, disease and illness in the body. True forgiveness is an ***energetic experience*** that occurs when we dissolve and release stuffed traumatic events that are stored in our energy fields. When we experience trauma and are unable to fully process through our intense feelings and emotions, we protect ourselves by shutting off the flow of our divine life force energy. We literally contract our energy fields, deposit our unprocessed feelings into a "deal with later" file and go about our day as if nothing has occurred. The stored energy from these traumatic events creates blocks and barriers in our energy fields separating us from the divine love, wisdom and healing energy of our God self. True forgiveness occurs when we are willing to process through our feelings and emotions from our "soul lessons" gaining the wisdom yet leaving the pain behind. Once our stuffed emotions and feelings get released, we re-open up space for divine energy to freely flow through our system allowing us to keep our hearts open. When our hearts remain open and we release all unforgiveness we have the *potential* to activate our high heart or thymus leading us into greater states of love, compassion and understanding. When we look back at paintings of Jesus, he is oftentimes pointing to the high heart area giving us clues as to where we need to focus our attention for healing, salvation and personal ascension to occur. Once the high heart is activated (it is an orgasmic event) we will have a direct experience with God and understand our unity with each other and the divine perfection in all things. Our consciousness will be expanded and we will realize that all souls are trying to balance misqualified energy and gain soul growth and understanding sometimes through difficult soul lessons. When we truly understand that everything that occurs in our life has been set up by our God self for our soul's advancement and evolution, forgiveness and compassion come naturally.

Unfortunately, many of us have given our power away because we have bought into the belief that Jesus has taken on the responsibility for all of humanity's sins or misqualified energy. This belief halts our spiritual growth because we don't learn the lessons behind our forgiveness opportunities thinking Jesus has already done all of the work for us. This belief fosters blind forgiveness and keeps our energetic imbalances, stored emotions and feelings stuck in our energy fields. We end up revolving in the same repetitive behavioral and psychological patterns lifetime after lifetime because we always react and respond from our stuffed emotional wounds that we have not released from our energy fields. Each of us needs to stop expecting Jesus to save us, he has given us the potential to save ourselves. Jesus seeded the planet with a higher consciousness activating the potential for each one of us to achieve his level of Christ Consciousness. All we need to do is clear out our energy fields and raise our vibrations high enough to merge with our God selves so we can activate our very own Christ Consciousness within our own being. It is our birthright….it is our divine mission!

We all want to take the easy way out, unfortunately, the only way out is for each of us to accept responsibility for our own shame, pain, unforgiveness, anger and fear we feel from all of the traumatic events that have occurred in our lifetimes. We cannot avoid what we have done to others or what others have done to us. We must move into our feelings and emotions and allow them to heal before we can truly forgive each other and ourselves. Many continue to say they have forgiven, but underneath their words there is a seething energetic eruption just waiting to burst. Many of us have masterfully constructed beautiful masks to place over our pain and we continue to hide behind food, alcohol, drugs, pharmaceuticals and escapism. We numb ourselves out! Many feel it is a waste of time and energy to truly express and experience their deepest feelings and emotions moving forward in their lives as if nothing is wrong. Energetically however, by avoiding our pain, we create layer upon layer of festering negative energy in our energy fields creating disharmony and disease in our lives.

Many of us have childhood trauma, pain and unforgiveness we have been carrying around for years. Childhood trauma is toxic and sets the foundation for our entire adult life. Those of us who have chosen to learn intense soul lessons from our families have a very difficult time forgiving our parents because we live in a constant state of fear. We have spent the majority of our childhood and adulthood not expressing our emotions or feelings because we are fearful of disrupting our families. However, in order to truly forgive our parents we must first access all of those old emotions and feelings before we can truly move into a state of genuine forgiveness. True forgiveness, letting go and releasing does not involve pushing away or suppressing our pain, it is actually a process of embracing our pain so we can integrate and heal the situation by coming to terms with it. We can only come to terms with something when we understand that each event that occurs in our life was chosen by our soul as a life lesson or experience for further advancement. Once we realize this, it is easier for us to release our emotional attachment. By allowing our emotions to surface, we can understand and integrate them helping us to dissolve our judgments about ourselves and each other. We can then move into a place of clarity and understanding, choosing to release our pain, while we retrieve the wisdom from the event that will help our soul grow. Once the lesson is learned, forgiveness is an essential step on the path to healing.

Forgiveness is a journey each of us must take on our own. It is the greatest gift we can give to ourselves! Many people do not want to forgive because they feel it will make the other person right for what they did. From a higher perspective, in God's dimension, there is no right or wrong. God is not in duality; humans are! However, there is energy balance and every person's action has a consequence. Everything anyone has ever said or done is recorded in the energy body of their soul and there will be a life review at the time of death. So instead of holding on to unforgiveness, resentment and blame allow yourself the time and space you need to access all of your stuffed emotions so you can release them. Forgiveness sets you free from the other person's energy so you have more space in your energy field for God's love, light, compassion and grace. When we hold onto unforgiveness we literally keep a chunk of that persons energy stuck in our energy field. This can create all kinds of problems for us because when our energy or life force is not able to flow freely we create blocks or energetic imbalances in our own system leading to all kinds of emotional, mental, spiritual and physical problems. Unforgiveness is cancerous to our entire system and it will halt divine union with our God self!

Keep in mind that our God self or Spiritual self is always with us, loves us unconditionally and would never allow anything to happen to us unless it was for our highest good. The quicker we set our intention to forgive, recognizing that our God self has brought us an opportunity for greater soul growth, the less likely we will find ourselves in a painful energetic entanglement with the other person. When we continue to hold negative feelings toward another person some of that energy gets stored in our own personal energy field and some of it gets sent to the person we are upset with. The universe will eventually return our negative energy back to us creating a destructive negative spiral. Whatever we put out always returns to us, so it is in our best interest to immediately disengage from all negative entanglements.

No matter how bad, how traumatic, how horrible or how damaging a person has been to you, set your intention to forgive and release them so you can free yourself. Forgiveness has nothing to do with them and everything to do with you. When we continue to hold grudges against others for previous offenses, the person we are really hurting is ourselves. However, forgiveness does not imply you must maintain a relationship with the people who have hurt you, especially if they continue to stay in the same state of consciousness that brought on the pain in the first place. You can forgive others and have compassion for them knowing that they are reacting from their egos and their lower state of consciousness and simply do not understand what they have done. In fact, stepping into your power, standing up for yourself, setting boundaries and choosing not to be a martyr may have been the lesson your soul wanted you to learn in the first place. Retrieve the gift each of these circumstances has brought into your life and step into true forgiveness, your most difficult and greatest soul's advancement!

Everyone is working from their own soul agreements, karmic contracts and forgiveness lessons. It is very important to surrender and allow the process while resisting the urge to pass judgment onto ourselves and others. We are all playing out our roles in a dualistic environment advancing our souls into mastery. When we allow ourselves to step into a place of unforgiveness and judgment we lower our vibration. Although some of us have had some pretty tough lessons, it should be our goal to move into compassion, release our stored negative emotions and feelings while setting the intention to step into forgiveness. Give yourself permission and the time and space you need to fully feel whatever you need to feel in order to release it. Eventually, we will all reach a place of inner peace allowing forgiveness to rise to the surface.

If you fall into unforgiveness, victim hood, blame and judgment recognize you are out of alignment with your soul consciousness and have fallen prey to your ego. Bring yourself back to your center, the truth of your being, knowing that there are no victims and everything is simply an opportunity for soul growth. The human energy field is very much like an onion and there may be many layers of pain and unforgiveness that will need to rise to the surface to be released. As these layers are cleared you may re-experience the pain and fall into blame. Simply recognize what is occurring, allow it to happen and choose to rise above it knowing that you are the co-creator of your entire life experience. Do not beat yourself up for falling out of alignment; embrace your humanity. Be aware you have slipped back into an old pattern and you have the power to step back into the higher vibrations of personal responsibility. When we are in resistance instead of allowance our negative mind chatter will intensify. This is an alarm for us to stop resisting and step into acceptance and forgiveness. Become aware of your thoughts, take several deep breaths and bring yourself back into the present moment aligning with your spiritual self.

Instead of looking at someone who has hurt you as your enemy, shift your focus to seeing them as your greatest teacher. Instead of being bitter, thank them for bringing you the greatest gift of all, the gift of personal transformation! Forgiveness is of the highest order and is the most difficult for most to master. Forgiveness brings you into a state of greater clarity and alignment with your soul helping you to release all pain, anger, regret, disappointment and frustration. There is one person in particular that needs the most forgiveness and that person is you! When you forgive yourself for your previous actions it will be much easier to step into a place of forgiveness for others.

- Forgiveness is a process! We cannot simply make a mental decision to forgive and let go. We must first process through the negatively charged energies that have held us in unforgiveness. Get in touch with your negativity. What emotions, feelings, fears are you experiencing? Write them down, acknowledge them, feel them but **do not** hold onto them! Ask God to help you release them.
- Write on a piece of paper the name of every person who has hurt you. Connect with your heart and speak to this persons soul letting them know you would like to forgive them and release them from any energetic entanglement that may have occurred. Once you have stated what you need to state, burn this piece of paper releasing all unforgiveness and pain up into the smoke returning it back to God to be turned into love. Repeat this process except this time bring into your awareness all of the beings you have harmed.
- State daily with your hand over your heart:
  I forgive you _____. Thank you for the lesson, we are free.

- Trauma gets stuck in our energy fields, muscles, tissues and cells and needs to be moved out energetically.

  Recommended Therapies:

  * DNA Theta Healing, Reiki, Sacral Cranial, Rolfing, Qigong, Emotional Freedom Technique
  * Massage Therapy
  * Psychotherapy (helps you get in touch with your emotions, feelings and distorted beliefs stored in your energy fields/subconscious mind.)

The weak can never forgive. Forgiveness is the attribute of the strong.

Gandhi

Forgiveness is freeing up and putting to better use the energy once consumed by holding grudges, harboring resentments and nursing unhealed wounds. It is rediscovering the strengths we always had and relocating our limitless capacity to understand and accept other people and ourselves.

Sidney and Suzanne Simon

When you hold resentment toward another, you are bound to that person or condition by an emotional link that is stronger than steel. Forgiveness is the only way to dissolve that link and get free.

Catherine Ponder

Forgiveness is choosing to love. It is the first skill of self-giving love.

Gandhi

We achieve inner health only through forgiveness – the forgiveness not only of others but also of ourselves.

Joshua Liebman

Relationships

Our most difficult relationships are our karmic relationships. These relationships are created with our soul mates specifically to assist both souls learn their lessons and balance their misqualified energy. When the lesson is learned, the karma is cleared and the contract has been fulfilled. Choosing to stay in these relationships becomes a choice. If both souls are willing to retrieve their lessons, step into a place of healing and shift their consciousness the relationship will evolve from one based on karma to one infused with the new energy of transformation. Unfortunately, both souls do not always choose to evolve and heal. Some souls will choose to stay in the old energy where they will continue to recreate the same lessons over and over again keeping them stuck in drama, trauma and chaos. They will cling to their old belief system, fear and ego and will refuse to open their mind to change. Each of us has the opportunity to expand our current level of consciousness and step into greater soul advancement but many will avoid moving forward and will get stuck in their soul lessons. It will be very important for those of us choosing to raise our vibration to not get caught up in other people's despair, confusion and denial. This can be very difficult to do because we care about our soul mates, however, we must respect their freedom to choose. Compassionate detachment and *discernment* are absolutely necessary if we plan on continuing with our own personal healing and the raising of our frequency. The one rule of all living things is our freedom of will and many of us have given our freedom of will away. We must learn to say "NO" when we need to and "YES" when we feel it is for our highest good. Each of us must learn to stand in our own power and learn to discern what is a good investment of our time and energy.

Staying involved in toxic relationships will deplete us and keep us from moving forward on our own soul's advancement. The only person we are responsible for is our self. Everything outside ourselves is merely a reflection of the relationship we are having with our own inner being. We teach others how to treat us by the way we treat ourselves so when we make ourselves of equal value and stop sacrificing our energy in order to please others, we will build a sense of personal power helping us to set up very strong boundaries. Keeping ourselves fully anchored on the spiritual path by choosing not to get caught up in relationships that lower our vibration is not selfish, it actually serves the whole of humanity! We cannot be of service to humanity if we continue to allow others to pull us down into the lower vibrational energy of confusion, chaos, denial, limited beliefs, addiction and drama. We need to pull ourselves out of denial and be really honest with ourselves and ask if our current relationships are based on love or fear. If they are based in fear, you will need to love yourself enough to disengage from anything that is dis-empowering and does not serve your highest good. This does not mean if you have made a mistake in a relationship you should take the easy way out and abandon it. You cannot change a negative behavior if you do not acknowledge it. Recognize your mistakes, bringing them into your awareness so you can transcend them. All mistakes should be immediately dealt with so the imbalanced energy will not be returned to you. The relationships we are speaking of here are the toxic ones where there is a split. One soul chooses to awaken and step into their empowerment while the other soul chooses to stay in denial and refuses to change and accept responsibility for their unconscious creations. These souls will no longer be a vibrational match and will only create continued disharmony for each other. It will be up to you to listen to your heart when it tells you your contract with another soul is complete. The only person who can decide this is you! You have total free will to choose which relationships serve you and which ones deplete you. Sometimes when we set a strong boundary with another soul and they see the changes we are making in our life it will prompt them to also make changes in their life. **Pain can be a catalyst for transformation!** If this relationship is meant to be a part of your life, give it the space it needs to heal. Release it with love knowing that it will be returned to you if it is for your highest good.

The highest way we can be of service to others is to stay in the higher vibrations of love, joy, peace, compassion, forgiveness and understanding setting an example for others to follow. One person holding their mastery core and radiating their energy can transmute the fear energy of hundreds of people who choose to keep themselves in limitation and fear. Set an example that others will want to follow. When we remain in the higher frequencies, we lift others up! Each of us will need to stay in alignment with our Spirit, listen to our hearts and choose not to allow other people's unconscious behaviors, motivated by their ego and shadow consciousness, throw us out of alignment with our spiritual core. Stepping into a place of detachment, surrender and allowance for our soul mates is absolutely necessary. They have free will and every right to choose to stay stagnant in their soul's evolvement. It will become imperative to look at everything from a bigger perspective, not a human perspective, and know that there is always divine order and a bigger picture in every event that occurs. We are all on different consciousness levels with the free will to choose whether we want to move towards the higher vibrations and divine union with our God Selves or stay stuck in the lower vibrations of limitation. Sometimes it takes others more time and many more lives before they will finally surrender their ego to their God self and move forward into enlightenment.

- Is this relationship, activity, thought or belief for my highest good?
- Is this relationship, activity, thought or belief a wise energy investment?
- Does this relationship, activity, thought or belief enhance or deplete my light?

- Do I wish to integrate this relationship, activity, thought or belief into my being?
- Does this relationship, activity or belief contract my energy through fear or expand my energy with love?

You do not need to be loved, not at the cost of yourself. The single relationship that is truly central and crucial in life is the relationship to self. Of all the people you will know in a lifetime, you are the only one you will never loose.

Jo Courdet

Karmic relationships are like a dance. When one person stops dancing, the dance is over.

Jennifer Hoffman

Every time our unconscious is working something out, it calls into our lives the people who have within the pieces of the answer we are seeking.

Martin Schulman

Knowing others is wisdom, knowing yourself is enlightenment.

Tao Tzu

Releasing Fear & Limiting Beliefs

Humanity has allowed fear to invade the consciousness of the planet, lowering our vibrations, keeping us from accessing the truth of our being. When our vibration is lowered our ability to hold light is diminished and our consciousness becomes polluted with untruths. All fear is based on the illusion that we are separated from God. Fear is not divine; fear is created by the ego. Our deepest fears are rising to the surface and are demanding our attention, transmutation and healing. At this time on Earth, we are each being presented with a choice as to which path we would like to choose. The path of light leads to unconditional love, the path of darkness leads to fear. There is no middle ground anymore, each of us must choose to either allow our fear to be a catalyst for transformation or we can allow our fear to consume us diminishing our light and halting us from moving forward on the ascension path. Freedom from fear and bringing our own Heaven here down on Earth is a state of mind that can only be experienced when we know with all of our being that each of us are a divine expression, an extension of God. We create our own hell here on Earth by allowing our egos to create blocks and barriers between our mind and God. Our ego "Edges God Out" making us believe that God is outside of ourselves somewhere in the sky judging every move we make. However, we could never be separated from God because God is the very source of life and without connection to God, nothing can survive. Each one of us is literally inside the energy of God and it is the energy of God that keeps every cell in our bodies alive.

Overcoming fear and releasing limiting beliefs based on separation is an essential part of our spiritual / ascension process. **Fear is one of the biggest obstacles each of us will have to overcome.** Fearful subconscious programming has been fed into our minds from the day we were born. Society, culture, family, religions, governments and media have all played a tremendous role in polluting our minds with destructive programming that separates us from our divinity and God essence. These systems have been manipulative, fear provoking, controlling, divisive, degrading and harmful to our souls. They have promoted ideas and beliefs that have literally enslaved humanity keeping us in a karmic cycle of death and rebirth. We have given our power away to dis-empowering beliefs that have halted our soul's growth from reaching its highest potential.

Fear of God and the belief in separation keeps us from merging into divine union with our God self. Overcoming duality, ascension and salvation cannot occur until our spiritual self has merged with our physical body. If our beliefs revolve around fear we will not be able to raise our vibration high enough for divine union to occur. Releasing all of our limiting beliefs and subconscious programming will be absolutely necessary for us to expand our consciousness into the realm of divine truth, not human truth. Our thoughts and beliefs are what shape our reality. Many of us were brought up believing we were born of sin. We were told God punishes and he is judgmental, controlling and demands our obedience. We were told we must overcome our flesh and our bodies were unholy. We allowed ourselves to buy into the beliefs of helplessness and powerlessness and began to seek someone or something outside of ourselves to save us so we could enter Heaven. Many of us still believe we have had and only will have one life to embody perfection just like God. The problem is, **we don't even believe in a perfect God**! Humanity has projected their *imperfect human characteristics* onto God never realizing that the God we choose to believe in is the person we will look up to and aspire to be like! The false God, the idol, we have created in our belief system is controlling, conditional, judgmental, separate, disconnected, angry, fearful, dogmatic and contradictory. Humanity has become just like the false God we have chosen to believe in.

The belief in a separate angry God simply is not true! God is bliss, boundless love, infinite intelligence, all-powerful, boundless wisdom, absolute harmony, indescribable beauty and *perfection*. How could we possibly believe otherwise? God is the source of all love and the creative energy that is in all things. God is the body of "All That Is", the consciousness of "All That Is" and the driving force that motivates and moves "All That Is". Each one of us are an extension of God and each of us has a direct line to our Creator. When we desire to connect with God, all we have to do is take the time to silence our minds and go within our *inner being*. We are never separated from God or from each other. We are all one. In the beginning there was nothing and God said, "Let there be light," and God said it was good. God created man in his own image and likeness. We are made of light energy, divine energy….pure consciousness. When the light vessel of God broke we all exploded into tiny pieces of indivuated light. Although it appears we are separate, we all come from the same source. Our physical form or body is our temple that houses our light and divine spark. Our body is what allows us to have the experiences we have in this dimension. We could not experience diversity, the beauty of a sunset or the miracle of childbirth without our physical vehicle. However, it is our physical vehicle that creates the illusion that we are all separate when in actuality we are one with God and all living things. We are individuated, diverse beings always connected to the Creator's energy of life itself.

It is important for us to remember who we are and release all old limiting beliefs and programs that are based on separation, fear and control. The only way to change our reality is to see it for what it is. We cannot create change if we are unaware of who we are. We are amazing, powerful beings. We are limitless. We can be anything we want to be for we are made of divine consciousness and we have within us the same creative abilities as the Creator. The only requirement is a shift in our thinking or a shift in our belief system. We are the creators of our reality. When we choose to create from our heart center, from a place of love, our creations are effortless. When we create from a place of fear we end up creating things we don't really want like illness, conflict, uncertainty, dis-ease and war. We are all magnificent, divine beings. We are divine sparks of God. We are capable of shifting our reality through our thoughts, feelings, emotions and images in our mind. When we begin to see ourselves as worthy, loveable, abundant, beautiful, eternal, joyful, balanced beings we will create that for ourselves. We are source energy, we are creative….it is important for us to become aware of our creations. We must stop looking outside of ourselves for the solutions to our problems. Stop expecting someone to save you! You have already been saved. Jesus the Christ took on a physical body so he could seed the planet with a higher level of consciousness. Each one of us, regardless of our man made religious "labels" are already Christed! Jesus activated the *potential* for each one of us to achieve his level of Christ Consciousness. It is already a part of our being; it is our birthright! All we need to do is claim it and activate it within our being by choosing to step into our empowerment and grounding ourselves firmly on the path of personal transformation.

Each of us must actively choose to release our distorted beliefs and conquer our fears in order to raise our vibration. When you run into fear, recognize that it is just a feeling. Fear is not who you are. Allow the feeling to pass through you and see fear as one of your greatest teachers. Fear teaches us that we have stepped out of reality and back into illusion. When we are in fear, we have fallen into separation and we have forgotten who we are. Humanity only has two emotions, Love and Fear. Every sub-emotion such as sadness, guilt, happiness, joy and gratitude falls under either love or fear. Fear (False Evidence Appearing Real) is the Ego (Edging God Out) and is based on the belief that we are separated from God. When we are in fear, we are giving our power away and we are not in the present or real moment. We have stepped into powerlessness and projected ourselves into the past or the future, the world of illusion. In order to conquer our fear all we have to do is acknowledge that "fear" is here and know that it is not real. Fear is always an illusion created by our egos. When you run into fear, resist the urge to deny or reject it. What we resist will persist. All we have to do is acknowledge its presence and choose to transform it into love.

People fear what they do not understand! Anytime fear shows up in your life, ask yourself: Where is this fear coming from? What am I going to do with this fear? What is my fear trying to teach me? Usually, you will be able to track it back to a distorted childhood belief based on separation and powerlessness that needs to be transformed and released. As you continue moving forward closer and closer to merging with your God self you will discover layer upon layer of fears that will have to be faced in order for you to advance. Each of us have *lifetimes* of stored fears within our energy fields that need to be transmuted and turned into love. This is a process and it will not happen overnight. The sooner we accept our fear without placing judgment on it and choose not to feed our fear with more fear the quicker our fear will dissolve. Begin to look at fear as your ally, as your greatest teacher and learn the lessons it is trying to teach you.

- Have you ever **really** thought about your belief system? Begin to question everything you have been taught. Examine any contradictions. Decide for yourself if it is really your truth.
- What are your beliefs about yourself? Are these your beliefs or are they someone else's beliefs that have been projected on to you?

- What are your limiting beliefs about yourself and others?
- What belief systems do you subconsciously hold that block your success?
- There are only two places to operate from, Love and Fear. When do you operate from a place of fear and when do you operate from a place of love?
- What beliefs are you willing to release in order for you to claim your divinity?
- In order to transform fear, you must first own it! Admit that you are choosing to experience the feeling of fear and fully allow yourself to feel it and embrace it so you can transform it. Shine the light of your consciousness on it and the darkness will disappear. Remember that fear is "false evidence appearing real". It is simply an illusion.
- When in fear, ask yourself, "Fear, what are you trying to teach me?"
- When in fear, state affirmations:

"God is here!"

"I AM one with God."

"I AM one with the Light"

"I AM surrounded with Gods love and light."

"I AM created from Love, I Am Love, I AM surrounded by Love."

"I have nothing to fear but fear itself"

"I release all fear and replace it with love."

Perceived separation from God and from each other is the cause of all your dysfunction and suffering.
Neale Donald Walsh

I would rather have a mind opened by wonder than one closed by belief.
Gerry Spence

The key to change is to let go of fear.
Rosanne Cash

The known is a prison. It is the unknown which is the field of pure potentiality, the field we need to step into.
Deepak Chopra

Courage is the mastery of fear, not the absence of fear.

Mark Twain

There's nobody out there. It only looks that way it's a trick. The conscious part of the mind looks out and sees all kinds of separation, different bodies and form, but that's an illusion. And the unconscious part of the mind, almost all of which is hidden, just the way most of an iceberg is hidden underneath the surface of the water, knows that there is really only one of us.

Gary R. Renard

The only way to define your limits is by going beyond them.

Arthur Clarke

Integrating the Negative Ego

Overcoming and integrating the negative ego is a central aspect on the spiritual path. As we just learned, it is our ego that creates fear. The ego creates a filter that distorts the way our mind perceives everything. It literally creates spiritual blindness and keeps us stuck in limited thinking. The ego places a veil of illusion or a veil of amnesia over our mind keeping us from accessing our higher wisdom and truth. Evil is the "veil" that blocks us from maintaining a strong connection with our God self. This veil creates the illusion that God is outside of ourselves. All external pathways that rely on a savoir or something outside of our selves to reach God is an illusion which has been created by the human ego. The only path that leads to salvation is the inner path. Divine illumination is given to those, who choose for themselves, to shed the illusions of the ego and reach for a direct relationship with their God self. Jesus clearly states, "The Kingdom of God is Within" and any teaching that teaches God is outside of ourselves is an anti Christ teaching. In order to enter the kingdom, which is the expansion of God consciousness **_within our own being_**, each of us must heal our shadow consciousness and transcend the human ego, which will lift the veil of amnesia from our minds. Once we pierce through the veil we begin to remove the darkness and confines of ego separation, denial and fear. We begin to see the light of truth transforming our denseness and darkness (coal) into vibrant divine energy (gold) leading us into God realization. Cleaning up our soul is an alchemical process and it is the very reason we incarnated in the first place.

Transcending the negative ego, raising our vibration and striving to expand our being into greater awareness is a life long journey. The ego will try to deceive us every step of the way because it does not want us to recognize who we truly are and step fully into our divine power. The ego will trick us into believing we have arrived spiritually. It will tell us we have learned all we need to learn and no longer have to work on ourselves. Spiritual complacency and the trick of the ego is very common in the Christian religion. We bought into the belief that once we are baptized, acknowledge that Jesus died on the cross for our sins and accept Christ into our hearts we are guaranteed salvation. Unfortunately, this has halted many of us from moving forward with our spiritual growth because we now believe Jesus has taken on the responsibility of our sins and misqualified energy. Our negative emotions, ego and shadowy psychological patterns get suppressed, denied and ignored because we believe Jesus is responsible for our salvation and we stop doing the inner work necessary to redeem ourselves. Believing in a savior outside of ourselves keeps us repeating the same karmic patterns over and over again keeping us in the pattern of death and rebirth in order to balance our energy. We have given our power away to something outside of ourselves to save us, accepting the illusions of the ego, which is a false path that will only bring continued suffering, chaos and drama! The only way to reach salvation and redeem ourselves is to go within our inner being accepting responsibility for our misqualified energy, soul wounds and repetitive patterns that keep us stuck in duality and separation.

Never underestimate the ego's power to keep humanity in avoidance and denial. The ego promotes psychological laziness keeping us stuck in dramas and difficult lessons so it can feed off of our energy. The only way to free ourselves from the trappings of our ego is to become conscious of it and do the inner work necessary so we can ascend our human consciousness up to our Spirit literally pulling our God self down into our energetic and physical vehicles. This will not occur until we become proactive in transcending our psychological wounds, repetitive behavioral patterns and are willing to balance our karma. An expansion of consciousness requires the willingness to self transcend. Self-growth and continued expansion never stops and is the very essence of creation. The Universe is always in a constant flow of transition, transformation, change and expansion. The Creator is always transcending itself into something bigger and better and our soul is expected to do the same. However, the ego and many religious groups, promote psychological laziness and comfortability so they can control us and keep us disempowered. If we connect with our God self, igniting the kingdom of God from within, we will no longer be stuck and disempowered. We will discover the truth of our being setting ourselves free from the control of anything outside of ourselves to be our source of wisdom, guidance truth and God connection.

When we choose to step into our power releasing the control and fear produced by the ego and fear filled organizations we will open our "spiritual eyes" and intuitive faculties keeping us from being blinded by the human ego. When our spiritual eye is not open, we are in the dark and literally cannot "see" the patterns and subconscious programs that continue to wreak havoc in our lives. When we are no longer blinded and we choose to open our eyes to "see" ourselves we will transcend our current level of consciousness and experience oneness with God and all beings returning to the ultimate truth, that God is love. In order to know God's truth we will need to *experience it directly* in order to release the confinements of our ego. We will not understand truth until it is experienced in that blissful state of oneness that occurs when our physical, emotional, mental and spiritual bodies have been cleared, integrated and balanced. When this occurs, our chakras will be activated and our energy fields will be harmonized and aligned in order for our God self to descend into our physical body. This is truly a remarkable experience, a mystical union that is available to all who are willing to "Know Thyself" and purify the misqualified energies in their physical, emotional and mental bodies. The spiritual body will begin to take dominion over our physical being and our God self will now be able to work through our lower being helping us to become the God empowered beings we truly are.

As we face God, we face ourselves. If we choose to serve our ego refusing to look at ourselves and our negative subconscious programs we will not be able to access a strong flow of spiritual energy from our God self. The only way to take dominion over the ego, gain health, vitality, right understanding and harmony is to build a strong foundation of God energy or spiritual energy running through our systems. This will amplify our energy fields and fill every cell of our body, mind and soul with the divine healing essence of God. This is an alchemical process where we turn our darkness into light. When we serve our ego, we look away from God denying our darkness, which creates additional blocks and barriers within our energy field. This keeps our vibration low and diminishes the amount of divine energy our bodies are able to pull through. A lack of spiritual energy is what creates all illness, disease, ignorance, bitterness and self-destruction on our planet. The human ego cannot be completely transformed until our God self has merged with our physical being filling it with its divine essence of light. We are multidimensional beings with our God self living in our higher vibrating dimensions (several feet above our head). We must actively pursue connection to this higher part of ourselves, through meditation, in order to activate our God consciousness revealing the truth of our being. Once our God self merges with our physical self, the real journey begins and our newly activated Christ / Buddha / Cosmic consciousness will empower us to see clearly through the illusions created by our ego. When we are willing to shed our pride and compensate for our past unconscious actions, face God and make things right, that's when we will take up our cross of karma and move forward into the magnificence of our being.

Raising our vibration, overcoming our ego's and striving to attain divine union with our God self is a lifestyle and a journey that will require self-love, patience and perseverance. Our ego is part of the human condition and it must be dealt with, acknowledged, balanced and integrated. The ego is very much like a rebellious child that is full of fear. The ego was created out of the soul's fear of perceived separation and the ego is terrified of giving up its control and surrendering to the love of the God self. Every time we make a decision from our God self we experience love, joy, passion for life, clarity, peace, fascination and fun. Whenever we make a negative decision from the ego we experience fear, doubt, control, unworthiness, powerlessness, confusion, denial and pain. The ego will tell the world how grand it is and what accomplishments it has achieved but deep inside the ego feels inadequate because it knows it was created out of illusion and not from the truth of our being. Any negative reaction, judgment or feeling we experience is always from the lower self or ego. Whenever our ego surfaces all we need to do is pay attention, become aware of it and observe it so we can transform it. We can take this opportunity to take dominion over our lower self and choose to respond from a place of love instead of fear.

Dedication to inner work and our spiritual growth is imperative for us to continually become more and more embodied by our God self. Refining and dissolving our lower being into a greater expression of who we truly are is a continuous process. The ego does not completely dissolve when our God self merges with our physical being. However, our God self will now have dominion over the ego or lower self and will *lovingly* and *patiently* guide our soul to release everything that no longer serves its highest good. As we raise our vibration, it is important for us to discern when we are working from our spiritual self and when we are working from our negative ego. The lower self / personality self is in duality and separation identifying itself as a physical body that is separate from everyone and everything else. It is based on fear and keeps us in a state of judgment, condemnation, separation and unforgiveness. Many people spend lifetimes struggling with their lower self never allowing their spiritual self to shine through so their lower self can be transformed. Our spiritual self is our truth; it is our divine self or divine spark that lives in each of us. It is this part of ourselves that urges us to see beyond our limited sense of identity. Our divine self knows we are more than our physical body and third dimensional titles we have put upon ourselves. Our spiritual self knows we are NEVER disconnected from God or anyone else.

Personality Self / Ego	Spiritual Self / Soul / God
Not recognizing the divinity in yourself or others	Recognizing divinity in self and ALL living things
Seeing yourself as separate from everything	Knowing you are connected to everything
Focuses on differences	Recognizes similarities
Intellect (Mind)	Intuition (Heart)
Hostility	Compassion
Re-Action	Awareness
Past or Future	Fully in the Present Moment
Fear (false evidence appearing real)	Courage
Judgment	Acceptance
Right / Wrong	Everything is an experience to learn from. Both negative and positive.
Better / Worse	Everything has value
Good / Bad	Acceptance
Separation Consciousness	Unity Consciousness

Personality Self / Ego	Spiritual Self / Soul / God
Outer Path	Inner Path
Belief	Knowingness
Conditional Love	Unconditional Love
Unforgiveness	Forgiveness
Blame	Personal Responsibility
Conformity	Authentic Life
Addictions	Freedom
Power & Control	Surrender & Acceptance
Dogma	Open-minded
Superior / Better Than	Empowered & Sees the Potential in All
Lack of Self Worth	Self-love
Elitism	Oneness
Compares Itself to Others	Sees Itself in Everyone
Fear / Darkness	Love / God's Light
Dis-empowering	Empowering

Personality Self / Ego	Spiritual Self / Soul / God
Chaos	Peace
Self Worth Sought through Materialism	Recognizes Self Divinity, Abundant with Spirit
Blocked	In the flow
Rigid	Flexible
Illusion	Truth
Co-dependent	Independent
Materialism	Spiritualism
Victim Consciousness	Empowered Consciousness
Doing	Being
Denies mistakes	Learns from mistakes
Defensive / Aggressive	Compassionate / Peaceful
Exclusive	Absolute Inclusiveness
Domination	Cooperation

Raising our vibration requires us to embody as many aspects of our spiritual self as possible. You will notice you have aspects of both the negative ego and the spiritual self. Humans are not perfect! Every human has a negative ego. We are here to learn lessons and grow from our current level of consciousness into a more expanded one. Oftentimes, we will make great progress and develop a very strong spiritual self.

However, the lower self is still a part of our being and it will reveal itself in very subtle ways. It is our responsibility to stop denying this part of our being and recognize when it overshadows our spiritual self. Self-awareness, self-honesty and the willingness to self transcend is all that's required to make progress. Our consciousness cannot be expanded if we choose not to look at our lower self ego and learn the lessons it is trying to teach us. There is always a lesson in *every* interaction! Self love and compassion for yourself, as well as, others is absolutely necessary while **we all** undergo the transformation of the lower self.

Keeping our hearts open during this transformational process can be a challenge. For many of us, the only way for our negative ego to be healed is for it to rise to the surface through a negative interaction so we can "SEE" the pain and trauma we create from our negative emotions, reactive behaviors and fears. Many of us have denied and stuffed so much negativity in our energy fields we aren't even consciously aware of what needs to be transformed within our own being. In order for us to heal our negativity we need to bring it out into conscious awareness, for all to see, so we can shed light on it and choose differently next time around. During this great transformation it will be important for each of us to surround ourselves around people who are actively working on themselves and transcending their lower self. If you look around the planet you will see a split between those choosing the light of knowledge and those choosing the darkness of denial. What we resist persist, so those souls who continue to stay in denial about their negative ego will continue to recreate the same toxic situations over and over again until they learn their lessons transforming their current level of consciousness into a more enlightened one. Everyone needs to obtain a heightened level of compassion for everyone during this process. However, that does not mean we need to continue to allow ourselves to become engulfed with repetitive negative interactions with others who continue to repeat the same lessons over and over again. Our soul mates may require traumatic events to trigger them into an awareness of the dead end directions of their old choices. Unfortunately, pain can be a catalyst for transformation.

Our heart is the entryway to the soul and our Holy Spirit. Because of this, continued traumatic events with those choosing to stay in denial could be counterproductive to our own soul's evolution. Have enough love for yourself and others to release all co-dependant relationships that are no longer a vibrational match. Many will choose to experience the duality and separation of the ego for an extended period of time. We must respect their free will choice even if we know it will lead them on a path of continued suffering and pain. For some, it may take many more lifetimes before they choose to raise their vibration high enough activating the Kingdom of God within themselves. Everyone has the same potential to connect to their heart space, the seat of their soul, their own personal Holy Spirit and reach up to their God self to incorporate more of its divine energy within their being. The ego does not want us to remember this and it will create a tremendous amount of resistance in our lives. In addition, the systems in our world are set up to promote the ego and do not acknowledge our true power. Overcoming our egos and the limiting programs we have created in our subconscious mind requires patience, desire, dedication and persistence. The egos greatest weapon is fear and denial. The Bible speaks of a deceiver that will trick many into following a false God. Unfortunately, many people have not realized that it is their own ego that deceives them into opting for the easy way out keeping them from doing the inner work necessary to further their soul's growth.

The majority of humanity has been in the grips of the negative ego / fear based / separative mind for the past 26,000 years. Our choices have created disharmony and unbalance on our planet, however, we are currently moving into the higher vibrations of soul consciousness, unity, unconditional love and peace. The Earth is ascending and we too have the opportunity to join her. It is a personal choice and we each have free will. We can choose to stay in our egoic limitations of duality and separation or we can choose to face ourselves and transcend our negativity by stepping into the love of our God self. We have a choice as to which part of our being we want to be predominant, the ego or the soul. We have to decide which part of our self is sacred and only allow it to be our source of authority. If we want to work from our divine essence we need to set our intention to reconnect with our God self. Our divine self has always been with us simply waiting for us to give up ego control and ask for its assistance. Everyday state:

" I surrender and release ego control and ask for my God self to merge with me and assist me with my highest and best good."

If you were still blinded by your ego you would have tossed this book away along time ago because your ego would have created a tremendous amount of resistance and discomfort fooling you into believing that this book has no merit. The majority of humanity is not even aware that they have given their power over to an imposter! The ego thrives on denial because it knows we cannot reclaim our power and heal ourselves if we are not aware of it in the first place. Many people's egos have such a tight grip on their being they are literally blinded from the truth of reality. Because of the powerful energies of the photon belt, many are just beginning to awaken and realize that there is much more to reality than what we had previously bought into. We have been like an ostrich with our heads in the sand. Those who have been so absolute and sure of things are beginning to rethink their old choices and are beginning to move into integrity accessing more of their authentic self by tapping into their soul and God self.

Integrating and overcoming the negative ego is a very intense process. Each of us will need to be very kind to ourselves as we dig deeper into our being allowing our hidden patterns and distortions to rise to the surface to be acknowledged and healed. We cannot heal something we are not aware of, so everything needing to be healed must rise to the surface! We must step out of resistance and into allowance. Because our egos have been in control for such a long period of time, it will take time to fully dissolve them into the light of God. Don't let your ego belittle you when you fall out of alignment! **The ego will build you up making you think you are superior and then diminish you when you make a mistake making you believe you are worthless.** Dissolving the power of the ego is a lifestyle! We all hold a tremendous amount of power within our being and because the ego is not based in truth, it can only maintain the power that we give to it. We are each powerful Creators of our lives! Who else could possibly be creating your world for you? We each have the choice and the power to dissolve our ego and change our personal world whenever we want to. When each of us accepts responsibility for the healing of our being, we contribute to the healing of the entire planet.

- When you notice your Ego has surfaced, ask yourself :
  What am I needing and why am I responding this way?

- Which part of your being is running your life? The Ego or the Soul?
- What parts of yourself are you willing to transcend?

God = Man – Ego
Sai Baba

Seek and ye shall find.
Matthew 7:7

I (the ego) die daily.
St. Paul 1 Cor. 15: 31

A Native American Elder once described his own inner struggles in this manner: Inside of me there are two dogs. One of the dogs is mean and evil. The other dog is good. The mean dog fights the good dog all the time. When asked which dog wins, he reflects for a moment and replied, "the one I feed the most".

George Bernard Shaw

Healing the Shadow

Our shadow is everything we think we aren't. It is an accumulation of our stored darkness that we refuse to look at and accept. It is everything we reject and hate within our own being such as our own anger, jealousy, fear, shame, lies, ignorance, intolerance, bitterness and re-activeness. Our shadow holds everything we think is "bad" and since we only want to accept our "good" qualities....all of our deepest darkest *secrets* get pushed to the background (stored in our energy fields) creating our shadow. Whatever we feel is not acceptable to reveal to our family, friends, society and ourselves is hidden within our shadow. In order to be accepted and feel good about ourselves we reject those parts of our psyches that we don't want to show the world. Unfortunately, all of these rejected aspects of ourselves still remain with us and are covered up by all of our social masks. However, these negative aspects are still a part of our being and they will continue to show themselves when we least expect it! Regardless of how much we try to suppress them, there they are seeking attention, healing and transformation. At a certain point on our journey back to wholeness, our shadow will reveal itself. What seemed like a straight path back to love, light and unification all the sudden takes an unexpected turn when the dark aspects of ourselves begin to make themselves known. At this point, we will no longer be able to hide from ourselves. As we face God, we face ourselves! All of our perceived "bad qualities" that we have not owned will rise to the surface so they too can be acknowledged and accepted and brought back into the light and truth of our being.

Facing our shadow is a difficult process because it appears suddenly, out of the blue, throwing us off track forcing us to face our fears, insecurities, past mistakes and poor decisions. Our shadow reminds us where we need to focus for a deeper level of healing. It shows us our repressed emotions, feelings, dysfunctions, history, denials, weaknesses, addictions and patterns. We do not need to fear our shadow; in fact, we need to learn how to embrace it. Our shadow will only show up when we are ready to truly move into wholeness, gain our highest soul's potential and become the master of our lives. **We must move through our darkness before we will truly be able to fully step into the light of our divinity.** When we acknowledge the information our shadow provides and accept its teachings, our shadow becomes the bridge between the darkness of our fears to the light of redemption and unification. Our soul knows when it is time to clear our energy and begin to live our life in a different way. When our soul feels we are ready, our shadow will be brought forth and each of us will be called to find the inner strength to face it so we can transform it. This part of ourselves can no longer be denied, it must be acknowledged, transformed and integrated into our being before we will be able to raise our vibrations to our highest potential.

When things in our life take a turn for the worst and we can't figure out what we are doing to create these circumstances, we can be sure that our soul has decided that it is time for us to meet our shadow. Our shadow is held in place by the unconscious parts of our mind that need healing. These unconscious parts are like sub personalities that were created from our unwillingness to fully feel our negative feelings because we perceived them to be bad. Since we have not been taught how to deal with these negative feelings, in a healthy way, we stuff them in our subconscious mind creating our shadow. This part of our self gets disconnected from our conscious self because we only want to deal with what makes us feel good. Unfortunately, the human experience does not always feel good and our uncomfortable feelings must be dealt with or we will continue to stuff things in our unconscious mind creating a darker, larger shadow moving us further and further away from the light of our God self. Denial of our negative feelings does not make them go away. In order to transform them they must be fully experienced so they can be acknowledged and healed. If we continue to avoid these unpleasant feelings they will continue to influence our behaviors and will be like little magnets that continue to attract people and situations into our life that we would rather not be involved with. When we feel like there is something outside of ourselves creating our life circumstance, and we want to blame others, we need to stop and realize that it is our shadowy sub personalities that are magnetizing these events into our lives. These parts of ourselves have been disowned and they are drawing attention to themselves so they can be welcomed back into our being and healed. This can only occur if we choose to receive the gift our shadow is trying to show us and acknowledge the emotion, feeling and behavior as part of our being. If we deny our shadow consciousness it will continue to persist. Bringing our conscious awareness to it and accepting it as part of our being shines light on it, transmuting it into love. Once all of these disowned aspects of our being are integrated, we will no longer need to draw unpleasant situations into our lives.

The unwillingness to look at ourselves honestly and make the changes necessary to evolve our souls is the essence of hypocrisy. We must accept accountability, responsibility and ownership of our own darkness and misqualified energy. We all have a shadow and the only way to transform it is to shine light on it through our increased awareness and willingness to stop rejecting those parts of ourselves that we don't want to own. Be aware that your shadow and negative ego support each other because they are both disowned aspects of ourselves that we have separated from the light of our God self. **Healing means to make ourselves whole**. By disowning and rejecting our ego and our shadow we fragment ourselves into separate beings keeping us from reaching a state of unification and wholeness. In order for us to re-member ourselves bringing us into a state of healing and wholeness we must recognize and own our shadow so we can transform our ego bringing more of our true divine essence into our being.

Both the ego and the shadow support each other because the main job of the ego is to keep us in separation, fragmented from our God self. In fact your ego will deny that your shadow is a part of your being, in any way. The ego knows if we recognize and heal our shadow, our shadow will be integrated into our God self which means the ego will be out of a job and integrated as well. In order to keep the shadow from being acknowledged, the ego will assist the shadow by helping the shadow to distance itself from its source of discomfort which creates further separation and denial within our being. For example, when we see someone misbehaving or being "bad" we pass judgment (ego) and immediately label it as "not us" (shadow). We blame (ego & shadow) and point fingers at everyone else for their inappropriate behavior projecting (ego & shadow) those parts of ourselves we have denied (ego) onto them making ourselves superior (ego) to all the other people out there (ego) who could never, never be reflections of ourselves. The ego loves to reinforce its sense of separateness by making us feel justified and self-righteous in our blaming. The egos basic premise is that of victim hood and a victim must always have someone to blame. Because our shadow avoids everything unpleasant, it will avoid taking responsibility for the co-creation of the circumstance and stuff it in the subconscious mind simply wanting it to go away leaving us alone. Unfortunately, this perpetuates and intensifies our darkness keeping our rejected parts inside the shadow and away from the light of our God self.

The shadow holds all the darkness from every traumatic event we have ever endured and not cleared from our subconscious mind. In order for us to fully step into our light, resolve our karma and raise our vibrations we must face and clear all of those things we refuse to accept about ourselves. This is why our relationships are often referred to as mirrors. Whatever we see in another person "that provokes an uncomfortable reaction" is usually a good indicator of a characteristic or sub personality within our own being that needs to be accepted and healed as well. We tend to see in other people all of the qualities that we have personally disowned. They are mirroring back to us our own shadows. Anger, hatred, jealousy and bitterness can only hurt us if it is denied. When we suppress our emotions and feelings, because we have been taught they are wrong, our shadow enlarges keeping us from accessing greater amounts of light. Once our feelings are embraced and we learn what they are trying to teach us they will no longer be stored in our shadows demagnetizing the charge they once had on us. For example, if we see someone overreacting and it doesn't provoke a reaction, emotion or feeling within our being, then we can be sure we have owned this aspect of ourselves because it will no longer have a charge within our being. We will be able to have compassion for this person knowing that a part of their shadow has risen up to the surface to be acknowledged and healed. Neutrality, not denial, is a good sign that you are integrating those aspects of your self that use to enrage you. However, if you continue to attract *repetitive* situations with people who keep demonstrating a similar type of behavior, that provokes a reaction in you, then you can be sure the Universe is trying to show you a disowned aspect of yourself that needs to be owned and integrated within your being. The Universe is lovingly bringing situations to each one of us helping us to heal and step into wholeness. When we have demagnetized all of our shadow consciousness, we will no longer attract relationships to show us our hidden aspects that we have been in denial about. We will no longer need another person to mirror our shadow back to us and we will naturally move towards those relationships that reflect back our light. Before we can be healed of any condition -body, mind or soul- we must be willing to take ownership of our creations before we can truly let them go releasing them into the light of God.

Each of us are affected by our own level of shadow consciousness and ego distortions. For the most part, this is not intentional, it is usually an *unconscious* act of self-deception that our shadow and ego thrives on. However, raising our vibration, merging with our God self and entering the Kingdom of God requires us to bring everything we have been avoiding unconsciously into our conscious awareness so it can be transformed. Energy never dies; it must be transformed! If we do not face our shadow, feel it and clear it we will not be able to raise our vibration high enough for our God self to merge with our being. We have to transform our darkness into light and the only way to do that is to bring it into our conscious awareness and look at it with brutal self-honesty. We need to clear out our energy fields and face our lies, shame, blame and anger. We must stop denying the negativity that lives within our being and face it so we can heal ourselves and become whole and authentic. These negativities are the very things we are here on Earth to heal. We are in a constant state of being refined and our ego and shadow work will not end until we have purified ourselves enough to be completely absorbed back into the light of the Creator Of "All That Is".

Shadow Reactions

- Anything that feels like it isn't you.

- Feelings and Emotions "others" provoke in you that you just want to go away. Your shadow is all of your rejections.

- All feelings and emotions you don't want to own.

- "Out of character" emotions or reactions that are showing up in your life. These are the hidden sub personalities, stored in your subconscious, that want to be healed!

- Aspects of your self you don't want others to see so you wear a mask.

- Our deepest, darkest and most terrible secrets.

- Our resistances. What we resist, persists.

Ego Reactions that Support the Shadow

- Blames others for their current situation. Refuses to accept responsibility for their own life / circumstances / creations / behaviors. We blame someone else when they exhibit a part of our shadow that is trying to be healed.

- Projects their disowned sub personalities onto others because they don't want to acknowledge their hidden issues. Finger pointing! Our outer reality is a reflection of our inner reality. Whatever we see in another person, that provokes a reaction, is a reflection of something within our own being that needs to be owned.

  " You are angry "

  " You are obnoxious "

  " You are over reactive "

  " You are hateful "

  " You are emotional "

  " You have a big ego "

- The ego creates the distance (separation) the shadow wants from its uncomfortable feelings. This creates separation / fragmentation within our being keeping us from reuniting with all of our parts, which keeps us from being whole.

- Denial! The ego denies that the shadow is a part of you:

  " I don't have a shadow "

  " I don't have negative feelings "

  " I don't have any darkness"

  " I don't wear a mask."

  " I don't have issues"

  " I don't need healing"

Signs You are Integrating Your Shadow and Ego

- You notice behaviors in others but have no need to react or respond.

- Other people's behaviors no longer create a feeling or an emotion in you. They do not trigger an internal alarm or create negative head chatter. You are becoming neutral.

- You no longer blame the other person or berate yourself when a shadow aspect shows up. You acknowledge and accept the disowned parts of your being, shining the light of your consciousness on them so they can be transmuted and healed. You are pulling yourself out of blame and denial.

- You are able to fully embrace and fully love all parts of yourself, even the parts that aren't so great. This is self-love!!!

- You embrace your humanity with determination and acceptance knowing that when your shadow consciousness arises this is a positive sign that shows healing is occurring in your life. You are allowing all of your disowned shadowy sub personalities to be demagnetized through your acceptance and healing of them.

- Your life has become more peaceful and your circumstances, relationships and interactions are becoming more positive.

Questions to Ask Yourself

- What judgments do you have about other people? These judgments show us our hidden aspects that need to be healed. Once we own them, other people's behaviors will not bother us.

- What scenarios in your life are repetitive? Do you keep attracting the same kind of negative people in your life? What are they trying to show you?

- Be really honest with yourself and make a list of all the things about yourself you try to hide from others. Recognize that it takes twice as much energy to hide these aspects from yourself and others than it does to own them.

- Where are you being inauthentic in your interactions? In what situations do you put on a "mask"? What are you hiding?

If we do not confront the darkness within us we will meet it as fate.
Carl Jung

Because the sage confronts his difficulties he never experiences them.
Lao Tsu

The gold is in the dark.
Carl Jung

When you can say, " I am that", to the deepest darkest aspects of yourself, then you can reach true enlightenment.
Debbie Ford

The unexamined life is not worth living.
Plato

Self Love

The greatest tool for overcoming the ego, healing the shadow, raising your vibration and transcending the human condition is to:

Learn to Love ALL of Yourself, UNCONDTIONALLY.

We are multidimensional beings with alter egos, sub personalities, conscious and unconscious aspects of ourselves. We are divine and human at the same time. A part of our being lives in perfection and complete union with the Creator of "All That Is" while another part of our being has fragmented and separated itself from the truth of who it really is. The only way to heal and return all of our parts to our truth is to love and accept every aspect of our being. When we truly love ourselves we will be able to acknowledge, accept and integrate everything we have ever been - both our dark and our light.

Until we truly love ourselves, we will never be able to truly express love to another being. Many people have a distorted view of what love is. Love is not a feeling; it is an emotion (energy in motion). Love is how we are behaving and interacting with ourselves and others, it is how we choose to carry our energy. Love is a state of BEING. In order to BE love to others we must first learn to BE loving to ourselves. Some of us are so full of fear we create chaos and confusion, not only for ourselves, but also with the very people we think we are being loving to. Love and Fear can never be experienced together; they are polar opposites. When we are in fear we are expressing the darkness and limitations of our ego and shadow consciousness. This creates fragmentation within our being, throwing us out of alignment with our God self. Many people allow fear to have such a tight grip on themselves, they end up sacrificing their own happiness in order to make another being love them. Their fear keeps them from realizing that their own lack of self-love will continue to create loveless, toxic relationships. When we stay in these relationships we are not doing our soul or their soul any good. These relationships are co-dependant and are based on *attachment*, not love, where each person feeds off of each other's negative egoic behavioral patterns keeping them stuck in repetitive cycles of low vibrational energies. Staying in these kind of relationships is not loving and will never serve anyone's highest good.

If someone is harming you emotionally, mentally, physically or spiritually the most loving thing you can do for yourself and them is to release them. Disengage yourself while you allow them to make their own choices even if you know their choices will create additional suffering for them in the future. Every being has a right to experience life in any way they choose, even if it means they are using God's energy in a destructive way. Releasing them does not mean you do not love them. Having the courage to set boundaries with these relationships and releasing them, if necessary, sends a message to the Universe that you are willing to learn the lessons involved and are no longer willing to dance this karmic dance. Setting healthy boundaries with others is an act of self-love and can also be a catalyst to the other person's soul to prompt them to make the necessary changes in their own being that could set them on the path of self-transformation. You can love them from a distance, while you use all of your energy for more constructive life affirming choices for yourself that will also benefit the whole of humanity. **Do not compromise the integrity of your soul!** Choose to be self-fulfilling and stop expecting someone or something outside of yourself to provide the love you seek. Unconditional love can only be found within yourself, no one else can give you what you already are. Go within yourself and activate it, feel it, be it. You are love!

Be loving and honest with yourself and release everything that no longer serves your highest good. Unconditional love is an *unlimited* way of being. Allow yourself to bring everything to the surface of your awareness releasing all of your limitations, illusions, out dated beliefs, negative patterns and relationships that interfere with your divine birthright to experience a life of love, peace and harmony. Each of us must evolve and heal our old ways of being so we can access our inner truth and beauty which is held within a deeper aspect of our being. As we truly discover who we are, we realize that the material world, humanity, our ego, our shadow, our parents, our jobs, our friends and physicality cannot define our magnificence. We discover our Spirit, our God self, the true essence of who we are, the very core of our being which is Love. By healing ourselves we are able to tap into our essence of love and it is only through the love of self that we are able to pull divine light into our physical body putting on our "garments of light" which activates our light body. When we are truly "BEING" love, we love every aspect of ourselves regardless of what is being shown to us or what we are creating for ourselves. We understand that all experiences whether they are negative or positive are self created and are blessings in disguise. We realize that pain has a purpose and if it is accepted and brought into our awareness it will provide an opportunity to learn, grow, change and explore. Denial is not loving!! Everything in our lives is a perfect opportunity for us to heal something, create something or experience something in order for us to awaken into the truth of who we are. When we are being love, we recognize that everything is perfectly aligned for the purpose of soul growth, which brings us closer to fulfilling our soul's journey. We no longer judge ourselves or place blame on someone else and their creations because we know that everything that occurs in our lives is divinely orchestrated to bring each of us closer to God. We realize that everyone is ultimately becoming the light and love of their true essence in human form.

Our light body, our divine birthright, cannot be activated until we begin to love ourselves enough to allow our divine energy to flow through us. Through our love for self, we will be able to transmute our denseness into light. Self-love, honesty and the desire to transcend the lower self will bring forth challenges, as all of our unhealed aspects of ourselves begin to be brought forth into the light of our consciousness so we can transform them. The only way to get through this process with ease and grace is to surrender to whatever comes up and love yourself unconditionally. The transmutation of negativity, painful experiences, distorted beliefs and trauma is sometimes uncomfortable. You will most likely re-experience the emotions and feelings that accompany the negativity so you can finally release them. Some of these experiences have been stored in our energy fields for many lifetimes and they are surfacing for a final clearing. The light of your God self is absorbing these distorted aspects of your body / mind / ego self that no longer serve your highest good. In order to become who we truly are, everything that is illusion must rise to the surface and be transmuted.

As humanity heals and transforms itself, it will be increasingly important for each of us to practice becoming observers of the situation by practicing loving allowance and compassion. As difficult as it is, we must learn to love every facet of ourselves as we allow and embrace all of our hidden sub- personalities, emotions, feelings, habits, negative patterns and illusions to rise to the surface so we can "see" them. If we are blinded by our negativity and don't even realize it is there how can we possibly transform it? In order to transcend ourselves and become the beautiful beings that we truly are we must first move through our darkness before we get to the light. Everything that is unembraceable, unacceptable, negative, "bad" is simply a distortion of our divine energy. It must be embraced with love by shining the light of our consciousness on it before it can be transformed.

Many of our current belief systems have set us up to reject our own Self-Love. We bought into the belief that humans were so "bad" and unlovable that God sent his "only begotten son" down to Earth to die a brutal death of crucifixion so we could be redeemed from our sins. We bought into the belief that God is an angry God who requested a human sacrifice to compensate for our "badness". This belief creates guilt, anger, fear, unworthiness, powerlessness and helplessness. It belittles the very nature of our being which is divinity and produces a perpetual cycle of self-condemnation. This belief keeps us from accessing a higher vibration and activating our high heart so we can feel God's presence within our own being. It creates separation and keeps us looking outside of ourselves for someone to save us instead of us accepting responsibility for our own distortions and misqualified energy so we can transform them. **Jesus did not come to Earth to die on the cross for our sins. God chose Jesus to come to Earth to be an example for us to live by and to show us the way to salvation.** Jesus came to teach us how to save ourselves. He came to empower the people to look within themselves for the beauty and power of God within:

"Behold, the Kingdom of God is Within You, Ye are Gods"

Instead of denying our distortions by putting on a false mask of "goodness," while we expect someone outside of ourselves to fix us, each of us needs to step into a place of personal responsibility and self love surrendering to our God self's desire to show our soul what needs to be healed and transformed. Our God self is just like a parent. If a child does something wrong the parent needs to talk to the child and show them what they did wrong so the child can self correct. If the child doesn't see what they did wrong how will they be able to learn from their mistakes? Each of us must be willing to honestly look at ourselves through the eyes of self love desiring to see everything within us that needs to be healed and released. As we face God, we face ourselves and if we do not love ourselves, we do not love God.

Learn to fall in love with yourself! You are a magnificent beautiful divine being no matter what you have done in your life. The true you, eternal spirit, remains in a state of perfection. Do not judge yourself or anyone else for things that have occurred in the past. Today is a new day and today you can make new choices. Make the choice to be loving to yourself and others even when the world tells you to be critical and harsh. Love yourself right where you are, right now, in this very moment. Allow everything that needs to be revealed to you, be revealed. Allow everything that needs to be released, be released. Allow all feelings that need to surface, to surface. Allow lessons that need to be learned, be learned. Everything that we have ever experienced as a human being is ripe for resolution and all we have to do is accept ourselves right now and surrender to the process of healing and awakening. Sometimes we expand our consciousness through traumatic events and seemingly harsh circumstances. However, from a higher perspective, there is great growth and beauty in these moments. We are like butterflies, emerging from our cocoons seeking out something new, something not so limiting, something extraordinary that propels us into greater expansion. Love yourself for embarking on this journey!

The only person who can truly love you, is you. You are an extension of God and you are made from the Creators Love. Most of us do great harm to ourselves by thinking of ourselves as less than God essence. We are divine God sparks. We are God manifest in reality. Allow yourself to tap into this reservoir of love deep within your heart and you will realize that no thing and no one outside of yourself can truly give you the love you are seeking. You are who you have been waiting for; it is your love you seek. When you begin to truly love yourself and remember how extraordinary you are, you will tap into the divine love of your God self. This is beyond human love it is agape love (spiritual love) and cannot be described with words. It must be personally experienced. When you activate this part of yourself all of your old rules and beliefs about yourself will disappear. Allow yourself to tap into your own dimension of love allowing the new you to be birthed. Embrace how incredibly powerful, unique and magnificent you are. When you remember this about yourself, you will begin to see it in everyone else.

- Many people use the word "Love" but their actions are not loving and speak volumes. Become aware of the areas in your life where you are "saying" all the right things but your behavior reflects something differently.
- Make a list of all the reasons you feel you are not loveable. Who helped you create these beliefs? Are these beliefs your truth or are they illusions you have bought into? Choose to acknowledge, heal and release everything from your being that is not love.

- Look at yourself everyday in the mirror and tell yourself how much you love yourself. Look in your eyes. Take note of your resistance. Look at your body. Give thanks to your body for being the divine temple that houses your spirit and soul. Look beyond your physicality; look for your divine essence that surrounds your body. Hug yourself and tell yourself how much you are loved.
- What beliefs, habits, relationships, negative thought patterns, activities do you need to let go of that don't support love for yourself or God's love for you. Release everything that no longer serves your highest good knowing that something better will be put in its place.
- Set your intention at the start of each day to utilize any obstacles as opportunities for growth. Choose to learn the most from each obstacle so you can avoid repeating painful situations and toxic relationship patterns.

Love without action is meaningless. Action without Love is irrelevant.

Deepak Chopra

You yourself, as much as anybody in the entire universe, deserve your love and affection.

Buddha

It is possible to undergo a profound crisis involving non-ordinary experiences and to perceive it as pathological or psychiatric when in fact it may be more accurately and beneficially defined as a spiritual emergency - a wake up call.

Stanislav Grof

Finding Joy

Being in a state of love, joy and gratitude attracts high vibrational energy not only to yourself but to everyone you come in contact with. It is infectious! When we are in this state, we radiate and ground our divinity and we activate more of our dormant strands of DNA. This is where God wants us to be, it is our divine birthright. There is nothing more powerful here on earth for us to do than to let love, joy, peace and compassion stream from our being. In order for us to truly allow and experience joy in our lives we must first be in touch with the value and essence of our being as an individuated spark of God. When we acknowledge the truth of our being, allow ourselves to heal the wounds contained in our emotional body, take dominion over the ego mind and connect to our God Self a *genuine* state of joy will flow from our being.

We cannot think our way into joy and pretend we feel a certain way while we deny and suppress the negative feelings and trauma circulating within our energy fields. Shifting our thoughts does have an affect on what we bring into our lives but we must also raise our vibration in order to attract what we most desire. Our dense emotional energies stay in our energy fields lowering our vibration and block us from attaining our highest expression of joy which can only be achieved when we are living in alignment with the truth of our being. In order for us to transmute our dense energies we must first get in touch with all of our feelings without placing judgment on them. When we feel our feelings we allow ourselves to have an emotional connection with our inner being and we find support from within! Our inner being, our soul, loves us unconditionally and connects us with our inner serenity! Serenity is when we "know" we are valuable and loved and we no longer seek for something outside of ourselves to determine our well-being, our goodness, our self worth. When we truly accept and nurture our feelings we hold ourselves in a sacred space honoring the value and essence of our being. Holding this sacred space for ourselves helps us to lift the veils of pain one layer at a time helping us to become more and more connected and filled with the divine essence of our Spirit. When this occurs, the increased flow of divine spiritual energy flowing through our system from our God self will dissolve our emotional blocks so we can tap into an authentic expression of joy, love, peace and compassion for ourselves and the rest of the planet.

Our beliefs also affect the level of our vibration. Each of us are on a journey back to wholeness where we heal our belief that we are separated from God. Our core beliefs of being cast out of the Garden of Eden, separated from the Kingdom of God and born into sin keeps us from accessing an authentic, true joy. Joy cannot be forced! Joy is a state of being and if we are not living the truth of our being, joy can never be fully expressed. Many of us have been living a false joy based on our false belief systems and the tricks of our ego mind. We fell into the traps of disempowerment forgetting how incredibly special we are to the whole of creation. Each of us are precious! We have forgotten who we are because we turned away from our spiritual center, our soul, which has always been fully connected to our God self. We have been living from the limitations of our ego's joy. We allowed our false joy to cover over our authentic joy by allowing ourselves to be nourished by things strictly in the physical world totally denying the importance of our spirituality! Material wealth, not spiritual wealth, became our focus and our souls are starving for abundance that can only be supplied through our Spirit.

The more we focus on bringing our God self down into our physical body, the greater our joy becomes. Abundance from Spirit cannot be supplied by anything outside of ourselves! Church, religion, governments, doctors, designers, spiritual teachers, books, healers etc… can not give us true joy! They may provide guidance, support and assistance but authentic joy can only be found through a strengthened connection with our God self. Each of us must choose to become infused with the Spirit of our God self and this can only occur when we enter complete stillness by turning off the ego mind through meditation. Every meditation brings in more and more of our divine spirit clearing away emotional blocks and traumas within our energy fields that block us from accessing our highest expression of joy. When we close off the cosmic life force energy from our Spirit we are not able to truly experience joy and we betray ourselves shutting ourselves off from our divine inheritance. Our ego mind, without an infusion of Spirit, lacks balance, compassion, access to spiritual truth and a higher vibration. When we are stuck in the separation of the ego mind we cannot access serenity because we are full of fear, doubt and confusion stuck in the world of illusion. Each of us has the exact same amount of potential, power and free will to transcend our ego minds and cultivate our own joy by choosing to reconnect with the wisdom of our soul and the unlimited love from our God self.

- Meditate. Enter a place of stillness every day. Allow your inner joy to rise up from the depths of your inner being. Joy is your true nature!
- What feelings do you have that need to be fully felt and released so you can free up space in your energy field for more of your joyful essence to flow through? Are you placing judgments on yourself about your negative feelings…this will halt you from being able to release them!
- Recognize when you have fallen prey to your ego and have fallen out of alignment with your joy, the very essence of your being. Once we have brought our Spirit down into our body, fully experiencing our highest expression of joy, our biggest challenge will be sustaining it in our everyday lives. A daily spiritual practice of meditation and going within your inner being will help you stay on track. However, if you fall out of alignment, take a few minutes to connect with your heart space, breathe in your Spirit and bring yourself back to center.
- Are you seeking approval from outside of yourself? Authentic joy comes from your soul, from your divine connection to your God self not from anyone or anything else! Get in touch with your feelings of lack and unworthiness, where did these feelings originate?

- Become aware of people, situations, beliefs and activities that keep you from your joy? Can these things be shifted and healed or do they need to be released?
- List ten "soul filling" things that bring you joy. Make time each day to do something that will nourish your Soul and Spirit.

Joy is a heart full and a mind purified by gratitude.

Marietta Mccarty

The process of facing and accepting all of our "selves" will bring peace, love, joy, harmony and happiness and fulfillment in our lives. As we drop our defenses and embrace all of who we are, we come to know our true identity as God inspired beings.

Susan Thesenga

The great teachings unanimously emphasize that all the peace, wisdom, and joy in the universe are already within us; we don't have to gain, develop, or attain them. We're like a child standing in a beautiful park with his eyes shut tight. We don't need to imagine trees, flowers, birds, and sky; we merely need to open our eyes and realize what is already here, who we really are- and stop pretending we're small or unholy.

Unknown

Where the mystery is present, joy is infinite; where the mystery has departed, efficacy is exhausted and the spirit disappears.

Ge Hong

Stepping into Your Power, Truth & Integrity

Stepping into your power, truth and integrity will require a radical shift in your thinking and great strength and courage. You will need to shatter the boxes of traditional thinking and release the old subconscious programs that have been projected onto you by your parents, friends, science, education, religion and culture. These distorted beliefs and subconscious programs, you have accepted as your truth, will sabotage you from being able to rise above the limitations, control and manipulation of the mass consciousness on this planet. Most of us were brought up and encouraged to give our power away. We were told what to think, how to dress, which friends we should associate ourselves with and which man-made religions would be imposed upon us as the ultimate truth. We grew up in a controlled environment disconnecting ourselves from our inner voice by buying into the belief systems that have been passed down from generation to generation. Rigid rules and behaviors became our comfort zone and the fear of rejection controlled us, keeping us from questioning those in authority. Our truth no longer came from our inner being; it came from an external source, robbing us from a deeper connection with our intuitive guidance. We became victims of circumstances forgetting that we are co-creators of our lives and we have the power and responsibility to transcend anything in our lives that keeps us from accessing the magnificence of our being.

One of the most tragic ways humanity has given their power away has been through the belief that Jesus the Christ died on the cross for our sins and that we are separated from God and each other. This belief perpetuates fear, shame and guilt keeping us from raising our vibration and accessing our higher wisdom because we are focused on an external savior and an outer approach to God. We attend church services on Sunday, follow the outer rules and doctrines yet deny our oneness with God and each other creating separation and disharmony within the very churches we attend, as well as, with the rest of humanity. All of our responsibility and power is turned over to the church to save us because we do not want to take on the difficult task of self examining our beliefs, attitudes and psychological wounds that keep us in a disempowered state of consciousness. The outer approach is based on the belief that we can enter Heaven by observing certain rules, doctrines and authority figures on Earth, as well as, the belief that someone outside of ourselves is now responsible for our misqualified energy or sins. This belief promotes spiritual complacency and goes against the Universal Law of Cause and Effect. For every action there is a reaction. Any misqualified energy we have created is our responsibility and can only be healed through our own personal inner work! Every word, thought and action is contained and recorded within our soul's energy field. The only way to heal our misqualified energy is to step into our power fully accepting responsibility for our own transformation. Each of us must set a deliberate intention to transcend our current level of vibration or state of consciousness into a higher one so we can actively clear out the accumulated lifetimes of misqualified energy stored in our energy fields.

This discordant energy can only be purified by the transformative and healing energies of our own personal and powerful God self. When we believe God is somewhere outside of ourselves we will never be able to merge with our God self bringing our divine spirit down into the earth plane. Each of us needs to take back our power from outside sources and reactivate our internal power by attaining a direct relationship with our God / Spiritual self. Through the inner work of meditation, the soul can invoke the healing energies of its God self to enter and activate all levels of its being transmuting the misqualified energy that is ready to be healed. However, the state of consciousness that created the misqualified energy in the first place must be acknowledged and transcended before our God self will provide the grace of transmutation and healing. Jesus clearly states, that unless our righteousness (meaning our willingness to self transcend) exceeds the righteousness of the scribes and Pharisees, we cannot enter the kingdom of heaven. The Kingdom of Heaven is a state of consciousness and it is found within a higher dimension of our own inner being. In order for us to enter we must transcend the consciousness of our lower self /ego and put on the Consciousness of the Christ. The Consciousness of the Christ knows that **each one of us** are sons and daughters of God. We are direct extensions of the Creator with a divine spark, located in our hearts, that is infused with the same creative powers as God simply needing to be activated. The Christ Consciousness knows that All is One and intimately connected. What one man has done, all men can do. The return of Christ is the "Christing" of any individuals that have raised their vibrations high enough to anchor in and activate their God /Christ / Buddhic selves into their physical bodies.

Jesus clearly states, "These things I do you shall do and more." Jesus the Christ was one of the most influential and amazing beings to ever incarnate into a human body and he came here to show us the way. He intended for us to follow his example, not put him up on a pedestal and buy into the belief that only Jesus could attain such a high level of consciousness. That belief is dis-empowering and keeps us stuck in duality and separation. Jesus is an incredible being that we are to aspire to be like. He is a son of God but so are each one of us. We are all one; there is no separation! EVERYTHING is a direct extension of God, EVERYTHING came out of Gods energy and EVERYTHING is always connected to God and each other. Each of us are responsible for our own salvation. We must take our power back and accept responsibility for the lives we create. We are powerful co-creators fully capable of attaining the same level of consciousness that Christ did! We each need to step into our power and go within the innermost part of our being seeking to attain *a direct experience* with God. When we connect with our God self, bringing our Spirit into matter, we allow God to experience this world through us. **This is our highest soul's potential to literally be so infused and closely connected with our God Self that our God Self and our Soul are both able to grow and expand.** That is the true nature of God, to transcend itself and become more than it was before. How can we possibly attain soul growth when we have disconnected and blocked ourselves from the very essence of divinity by believing that something outside of ourselves can give us God?

Stepping into your power, truth and integrity means that you will no longer allow others to do your thinking for you. When you commit yourself to meditation, seeking the kingdom within, you will expand your consciousness and have a greater knowing of higher truths. The more you meditate, the higher your vibration will rise and the clearer your energetic fields will become. Cloudy energy fields interfere with clear guidance and keep you from accessing a higher vibration. As your energetic blocks are cleared, guidance from your God self will become easier. It will take time, practice and faith to reach such a point of clarity. Trust yourself and honor yourself for staying open to the expansion of your higher consciousness! Allow yourself to evolve into deeper truths and a heighten connection to your divine essence. **The higher your vibration the higher level of truth will be revealed to you.** Ultimately, your level of truth is based on your level of consciousness. Unfortunately, many people have bought into the truths of certain organizations and they feel they know it all. This leads to a contracted, limited state of consciousness that keeps people from growing and expanding. Resist the urge to fall into this trap! You have a built in ability to know truth, to know what is the right thing to do. Only you can know what is right for you! This kind of knowingness is beyond the intellect and the rational mind (ego), this kind of knowingness comes from the heart (soul). Tap into your soul consciousness, trust yourself and follow your own truth!

God gave you the freedom to pursue your own unique path and it is up to you to reclaim your divine birthright to create the life you want. Organizations that force us to live and act the same, according to their rules, interferes with the Creator's will of diversity. Although we are all connected and made from source energy we created ourselves to each be on a different life path so God could experience himself in a variety of ways. Why would God want us to all be and do the same thing? However, there is only one way for us to reach the kingdom of God and that is through ourselves! It does not matter which man-made religion we have bought into! What matters is our desire and willingness to transcend our lower selves so we can expand our consciousness and have a direct experience and relationship with God through the activation and healing of our soul. Jesus stated, "I AM the way and the only way to my Father." He knew that his Father could be found *within* his own being. There are a multitude of organizations that can assist you on your pathway back to God and they are the ones based on unconditional love, unity, forgiveness, compassion, acceptance and peace. However, make sure you do not give your power away to these organizations! They may be able to lead you in the right direction and provide comfort, but ultimately it is **you** who must do the *inner work* to connect with your God self. Any organization that does not honor the divinity within **every** being and is based on fear, sin, hierarchy, disempowerment, separation and judgment is not in alignment with the love and truth of God.

Set your intention to step back into your power releasing all disempowering activities, beliefs and subconscious programs that keep you from truly accessing and remembering who you truly are. No one can save you but you. **YOU** are the most powerful force in your life and no one can deprive you of this power unless you allow them to. God gave you the freedom to pursue your own unique path and it is up to you to reclaim your divine birthright to create the life you want. Step into your power, be courageous and stop allowing other people to make decisions for you. Choose to live from the center of your being and become the director of your own life. Do not allow other people's opinions, judgments, criticisms and beliefs deter you from living your own authentic, divinely aligned life. Be true to yourself and release all people, places and things that do not empower you. You are a divine spark, a piece of God, and no one but you and God knows what is best for you. Friends, Family, Spiritual Teachers, Books, Classes etc… can be of great assistance and point you in the right direction, however, you must be very vigilant in not giving your power away to external sources. Your power and truth lies within, don't allow anyone or anything to ever get in the way of your divine right to choose. As Jesus said:

"These things I do you shall do and more." (John 14:12)

"Neither shall they say, lo here, lo there, for behold the Kingdom of God is within you." (Luke 17:21)

"I and my Father are One." (John 10)

"Ye are Gods." (John 10)

"Dare to put off the old man (ego) and put on the new man (Christ self)." (Ephesians 4: 22-24)

- God experiences and creates through us. Is your life what you want God to experience?
- Where do you give your power away? Family, Friends, Work, Church, Government, Doctors, Your Ego, Your Attachments, Your Addictions?
- In what places do you try to control people? In what places do you allow others to control you?
- Do you live from your heart (love) or your mind (fear)?
- Take the time to go within and seek to "experience" a deeper connection with your God self.
- Do the organizations, activities and events you attend make you feel good? Do you leave with a sense of peace, love and upliftment or do you leave with a feeling of disempowerment, fear, shame or guilt? Did the message or lessons express your greatness? Was your highest good served by participating with this organization, activity or event?

Great Spirits have always encountered violent opposition from mediocre minds.

Albert Einstein

A new idea is first condemned as ridiculous and then dismissed as trivial until finally it becomes what everybody knows.

William James

Inaction is an action in itself.

Deborah Lowrey

The mind once expanded to the dimensions of a larger idea never return to its original size.

Oliver Wendell Holmes

Actively Meditating

Meditation is the fastest way to raise your vibration, get in touch with your feelings and emotions and connect more strongly with your God self. **The real you is not the physical you! The real you is Eternal Spirit!** Your physical body houses a part of your Spirit but the real you lives in and around your physical body and *exists in many dimensions.* Each of us are incredibly vast multidimensional beings with a very small part of the real us in our physical body. In order for us to move into wholeness, we need to bring *more* of our true essence into our physical body by clearing the pathways between our physical self and the energetic layers that surround the physical body. Our energetic fields contain emotional and mental blocks and traumas from this lifetime and previous lives that need to be healed and cleared. These blocks inhibit the abundant flow of spiritual energy coming from our God self, therefore, limiting the expansion of our consciousness keeping us stuck in repetitive patterns lifetime after lifetime. Once these blocks are removed, personal ascension can occur. Personal ascension is when you have cleared your energetic layers and lifted your consciousness, your frequency or your vibration high enough so your Spirit can descend into matter (your physical body).

True healing is not physical/mental healing. True healing is Spirit/Soul/Energetic healing. Many of us have built up walls shielding ourselves from the enormous amount of love, truth and peace our God self wants to provide for us. Our spiritual self is where we can access vast amounts of information about others, the universe, God and ourselves. Once we tap into this portion of ourselves we will be able to reclaim our full power and divine guidance. Once each of us merges with our God self we will operate from a place of divine love and alignment. We will no longer seek answers from outside of ourselves and we will become God realized beings. We will tap into our divine super consciousness and be able to retrieve the information and guidance we need in order to live our highest life potential. When everyone on the planet is living from a place of total connection with their spiritual self everyone will operate from a place of unconditional love, joy, compassion, gratitude and peace. Fear, control, victim consciousness, powerlessness and helplessness will be a thing of the past.

Many people avoid taking the time for meditation, inner contemplation and silence because this is where the things that need to be healed…. mainly our inner beliefs, negative thoughts, fears and emotions are stored. Oftentimes, we are fearful of truly connecting with our inner being because we are afraid of what we might discover. However, going within is the only way we will find the coal we need to turn into gold. It is an alchemical process where we turn our low vibrating denseness (coal) into higher vibrational light (gold). This is a process we must undertake in order to become whole and at peace within ourselves and the world. We cannot avoid our negativity, pain and trauma. We must move into our darkness and transmute it before we are able to fully step into our light. The most effective way to heal ourselves is by connecting with our Spirit and integrating all of those aspects of ourselves we have disowned. All of our baggage (negative feelings, anger, resentment, judgments, fears and insecurities) must be acknowledged before we can heal them. In order to get in touch with them, we must still our minds through meditation. Prayer is also a very powerful way to set a strong intention and ask for assistance. However, prayer *alone* does not reach into the deeper levels of our subconscious because our mind is very active "speaking" to God. Meditation quiets the mind penetrating the deeper aspects of our being enabling us to "hear" messages from our God self activating portions of our brain that helps us heal. **Prayer combined with meditation is a power packed healing combination.**

Meditation brings in divine life force energy revitalizing our energetic and physical bodies. Just because most people can't see energy or their energetic body does not mean it's not there. Even if you can't see energy, you can FEEL it. Our invisible fields are just as important as our physical body. In fact, it is our energetic fields that shape and hold in place our physical body. At death when our Spirit /Energetic body leaves our physical body, the body immediately begins to decompose.

Unfortunately, many of us are only aware of our physical being and aren't aware of the incredible wisdom, healing and power our energetic body contains. This lack of knowledge leads us to treat our bodily symptoms strictly from a physical perspective using a band-aid approach. We seek out as many man made chemical medicines, surgeries and quick fix remedies we can find avoiding the real cause of our pain and dis-ease. All illness begins in our energy fields first and if left unattended will eventually manifest itself in the physical body. Once the energetic imbalance is embedded in the energy field and moves through all energetic layers of the energy body it will introduce itself as a pain, ailment, physical illness or disease. All symptoms and illnesses arise to warn us that something within our being - emotional, mental, spiritual or physical - is out of balance. It is imperative for us to bring into our awareness the truth of who we are so we can incorporate energetic / spiritual healing *in combination* with physical healing.

Meditation, with your intention to heal, literally brings the Light of God and large amounts of life force energy into your being. This light transforms, heals, energizes, brings awareness, expands your consciousness, raises your vibration and connects you to the divinity in yourself and everyone else. You will find your truth, freedom and healing internally. Only God can give you God and God is found within yourself. No other person, church or organization can give you what you are seeking. Choose to become a seeker of self and you will discover how incredible you truly are. Meditation is your journey to en-lighten-ment. When Jesus and Buddha were incarnated they were initiated with powerful Light from God to assist them on their path of awakening all. Their great power, belief and faith were increased 1000 fold by the Light energy. Jesus said, "These things I do you shall do and more". Each of us carries a divine spark of God light in our hearts that we can expand! God loves us so much he gave us free will to make our own choices. We can choose to be a dim sputter of light or we can choose to actively allow the light to grow, through meditation, becoming powerful light conductors just like Jesus and Buddha. Even the darkest of beings still have God's light in their heart. Without God's light we cannot survive. Every being no matter where they are on their journey can decide to receive more light and the best way to do that is to actively meditate. See the light, feel the light, use the light…bring it in. It surrounds us, is a part of us and loves us. It is God's gift to each one of us. Make the choice to receive it, expand it and express it. As Gandhi says "We need to BE the light we wish to see in the world."

Benefits of Meditation

1. Daily meditation brings in the healing light of God. This light penetrates the physical, emotional, mental and spiritual energy fields helping us dislodge stagnant blocked energy that leads to imbalances, disease and the illusion that we are separated from God.
2. Every time we meditate we bring in *more* and *more* of our God Self.

3. God (Light) comes in through us gradually. The density of our form *lessens* and *lessens* with every meditation becoming *more* and *more* filled with the Spirit and Light from our God self.

4. Meditation realigns the energy fields with the divine order of the universe deepening and strengthening our connection to Source.

5. During meditation, the light of our God self moves through the physical body assisting in the healing of all organs, tissues, blood and bones. Meditation reduces pain!

6. Meditation improves blood pressure, reduces anxiety, decreases muscle tension and headaches, enhances the immune system, increases serotonin for better moods, improves depression and relieves emotional distress.

7. Meditation quiets the mind, allowing us to receive *clear* divine guidance and tap into the greater depth of who we are. It is in the very positive mental states of our Theta and Beta brainwaves that we are able to move beyond our human consciousness into our God Consciousness. This is an ideal state for healing and transformation!

8. Meditation expands our consciousness, raises our vibration and helps us remember who we are.

9. Meditation helps us stay calm and less reactive when we encounter difficult situations.

10. Meditation opens, clears and aligns the chakras for a greater sense of health and well-being.

11. Meditation balances and calms the nervous system.

12. Meditation balances the left (masculine: logic, power, reason) and right (feminine: creative, love, intuitive) sides of the brain. Both sides need to be balanced to clear away the negative ego so we can have a direct experience with God. People are usually dominant on one side. Bringing both sides of the brain into balance also balances the energetic bodies and helps us move out of dualistic thinking.

13. Meditation assists people overcome addictions and repetitive negative patterns.

14. Meditation helps us assimilate the powerful energies coming into the planet from the galactic center. These energies are activating our light codes, DNA, cellular memory and are assisting us move into the golden age with ease and grace.

15. Meditation assists us in rising above the subconscious programming of the mass consciousness so we can release all dis-empowering thought forms that keep us from activating our divine potential.

99% of a person is invisible and untouchable.
Buckminster Fuller

Meditation is the tongue of the soul and the language of our Spirit.
Jeremy Taylor

If you want to find God, hang out in the space between your thoughts.
Alan Cohen

If you meditate, sooner or later you will come upon love. If you meditate deeply, sooner or later you will start feeling a tremendous love arising in you that you have never known before.
Osho

Meditation Exercises for Transformation

Meditation and Visualization are powerful tools for healing and transformation! Creation is a thought in the mind of God. We are made in the image and likeness of God, therefore, we have the same creative powers as God. We must continue focusing on what we want to create in our lives! That's why visualization is so important because it trains our mind to take our thoughts and put them into words and pictures. When we think about something, see it in our minds eye (visualize it) and allow ourselves to believe and *feel* it is occurring we create exactly what we are focused on. That's how powerful we are! **Visualization is real**, do not let the ego mind trick you into believing this is fantasy.

Bringing in the Light (10 Minute Beginners Meditation)

1. Find a quiet place. Sit under a tree, lie on your bed or sit in your car. Make sure your spine is straight. It doesn't matter where you are the light is always with you.

2. Close your eyes and ask God to surround you with his love and healing light. See your self surrounded and immersed in a bubble of white light.

3. Slowly take a minimum of **TEN** deep breaths filling your lungs to capacity and HOLD until you need to exhale. Deep breathing helps you enter into an altered state of consciousness and helps you relax. Deep breathing is very important and is an essential component to helping you connect to your soul getting the most out of your meditations.

4. Visualize a gold or white ball of light above your head. This is where your God self resides! Do not allow yourself to get hung up on the specifics of visualization. Whatever you visualize is what is right for you.

5. State your intention OUTLOUD:

"I ASK AND INTEND TO CONNECT WITH MY GOD SELF AND RECEIVE THE PRESENCE OF GODS HEALING LIGHT."

6. See the light of your God self entering and filling the top of your head, moving down your face, neck, shoulders, arms, heart, stomach, pelvis, legs and out your feet into the Earth.

7. See yourself filled with Gods light and bask in it for as long as you like. Focus on the light, releasing all thoughts. Allow yourself to just "BE". The longer you allow yourself to meditate the more relaxed you will become and the more likely you will be able to access a very positive mental state of Alpha and Theta brainwaves.

8. If you have areas in your physical body that need additional healing, you can focus your consciousness in that area filling it with additional light *intending* it to be healed.

9. When you are ready, give thanks to God for sharing his/her love and healing light.

Commit yourself to doing this meditation EVERYDAY. This meditation does not have to take a lot of time. I recommend 10-15 minutes a day to begin with. Everyone can find ten minutes out of their day to commune with their God self. Don't let your ego make excuses! Like everything, visualization and meditation takes time to get use to. Obviously, the longer you stay in a meditation the greater the results. Make the decision to do this meditation everyday for one month. By the end of the month, it will not require as much focus and it will begin to come naturally. You will actually look forward to your quite time with your Spirit. You will also begin to notice subtle changes in your moods, emotions, ability to concentrate, reasoning skills and an overall since of inner peace.

In the beginning you may have thoughts racing through your mind, you may doubt or question the process. You may think this is silly, abnormal and a waste of your time and you may run into fear because you have never done this before. You may even think you are doing something wrong! This is completely normal. Don't focus on it, allow these thoughts to surface and release them. Your egoic mind will try to tell you this is a waste of time because it knows meditation will bring your Spirit and ego into balance and your ego does not want to give up control! You cannot do anything wrong when you begin to meditate. Whatever occurs is suppose to occur and is part of you surrendering to your God Self and relinquishing your ego.

It takes time to train the mind to sit in silence. After your 10 minute meditation you can practice 3 minute fast-fix meditations throughout your day to keep you balanced and centered. The more you put into it the more you will get out of it. Your fast-fix meditations can bring in the light while sitting in the doctors office, waiting for the kids in the car pick up line, on your lunch break, before you get out of bed in the morning, during TV commercials, before you go to bed at night or when you have fallen off center due to some sort of upset. It doesn't matter where you do it - just do it.

Meditation Tips

1. Wear loose, comfortable clothing and make sure you are hydrated.

2. Lie down or sit up. Divine energy flows through the spine so make sure it is straight. Do not bow your head, it will cut off the flow of divine spiritual energy!

3. Light incense or mist your space with essential oils or aromatherapy. Although this is not necessary, scent can greatly enhance your meditation and help you quite your mind reaching an altered state of consciousness.

4. Music quickly alters your state of consciousness, raises your vibration and helps you to quickly enter into Theta and Beta brainwaves. Portable earphones work better than overhead music. Hemi Sync cd's are produced specifically for meditation and help balance the right and left sides of the brain.

Holy Breath Meditation

1. Lie down or sit in a chair with your spine straight.

2. Close your eyes and set your intention to connect with your divine self.

3. Focus your attention several feet above your head.

4. Take a slow deep breath through your nose visualizing white light entering through the top of your head and moving into the center of your heart.

5. When you exhale, push this light out through your heart releasing all sadness, stuck energy, pain, insecurity, grief and fear. This light may turn gray as you blow it out from your heart center.

6. Repeat 20 times or as many times as you feel comfortable.

This meditation will help you focus on bringing in large amounts of the "breath of life". Deep breathing is essential because it connects us to our still point helping us to access the greater part of our being that is fully connected to All-That-Is. Our breath is like the wind cleaning and clearing away old structures, patterns, erroneous beliefs and stagnant energy. The wind and our breath are transformative. Breathing deeply lifts our spirit and moves us into a peaceful state of consciousness. When we do the holy breath meditation we breathe in prana or life force energy assisting us to clear out our cells and revitalize our blood. Deep breathing also raises our vibration, clears our emotional and mental states, reduces blood pressure, helps us reach deeper states of awareness and helps us to relax and connect to our divine self. We are God in form! The idea that we are separate from God is the root of all of our suffering. When you forget this and feel overwhelmed, breathe and remember who you truly are. Deep breathing can help you realign your life with your highest intention.

Emotional Release Meditation

This is a great meditation to do when you have a lot of emotional baggage you need to release. The "bubbles" represent our stored pain, feelings and emotional wounds - allow them to rise to the surface for transmutation. This meditation is also helpful after you have been in conflict with someone and you need to bring yourself back to center.

1. Lie down or sit in a chair. Keep your spine straight. Close your eyes and take three deep breaths. Ask God to surround you with his love and healing light. See yourself surrounded and immersed in a bubble of white light.

2. State your intention:

" I ask for all things that no longer serve my highest
good to be released with ease and grace"

3. Bring into your awareness all of the people, events, feelings and circumstances needing to be released.
4. Allow yourself time to engage yourself with the feelings of each circumstance one at a time.
5. Visualize a bubble rising out of your heart. Label this bubble with the name of the person, event, feeling or circumstance that needs to be released.
6. Watch this bubble float up away from you and up into the sky. See this bubble going up to God. Visualize God filling this bubble with white light transmuting it back into love.
7. Repeat this process until everything that needs to be released is healed. If an event has been deeply traumatic, you may need to repeat this process several times in future meditations. Setting a strong *intention* to release and allowing yourself to truly "feel" the feelings involved will greatly enhance your ability to move on quickly with ease and grace. If we ignore or deny our feelings we hold onto them.
8. Once you feel you have released everything that is ready to be released, visualize yourself and the person, place or event involved standing across from each other. See each of you surrounded by white light. State in your mind: "All is forgiven and we are each set free".

Basic Chakra Meditation

1. Find a quiet place. Lie down or sit with your spine straight.
2. Close your eyes and ask God to surround you with his love and healing light. See yourself surrounded and immersed in a bubble of white light.
3. State your intention OUTLOUD:

" I ask and intend for my chakras to be cleaned out,
aligned and balanced."

4. Visualize a white ball of light above your head. See the light filling and entering the top of your head.
5. See this white light move to your spiritual eye center in between your eyebrows. See your spiritual eye turn a beautiful **Indigo** color.

6. Visualize a hot fiery white light moving into your spiritual eye. Ask this light to clean and open your spiritual eye chakra. Return your spiritual eye to **Indigo**.

7. See this white fiery light move down your face into your throat chakra. See your throat chakra turn a beautiful **Blue** color. Visualize a hot fiery white light moving into your throat chakra. Ask this light to clean and open your throat chakra. Return your throat chakra to **Blue**.

8. See this white fiery light move down both arms and out the palms of your hands. Visualize it moving back up your arms and into the heart chakra. See your heart chakra turn into a beautiful **Green** color. Visualize a hot fiery ball of white light move into your heart chakra. Ask this light to clean and open your heart chakra. Return your heart chakra to **Green**.

9. See this white fiery light move slightly below your ribcage or solar plexus chakra. See your solar plexus turn a beautiful **Yellow** color. Visualize a hot fiery white light moving into your solar plexus. Ask this light to clean and open your solar plexus chakra. Return your solar plexus chakra to **Yellow.**

10. See this white fiery light move down to your belly button area or sacral chakra. See your sacral chakra turn a beautiful **Orange** color. Visualize a hot fiery ball of white light moving into your sacral chakra. Ask this light to clean and open your sacral chakra. Return your sacral chakra to **Orange**.

11. See this white fiery light move down to the base of your spine or root chakra. See your root chakra turn a bright **Red** color. Visualize a hot fiery white light move into your root chakra. Ask this light to clean and open your root chakra. Return your root chakra to **Red.**

12. See this hot fiery white light move down your legs and out the soles of your feet deep into the Earth. Visualize energetic roots growing out of the bottom of your feet deep into the center of the Earth. Empty your mind and allow yourself to stay in this meditative state. When you are ready to return, review your chakras once again. This time visualize white light from the Earth moving into the soles of your feet, up your legs to your **Red** Root Chakra, up to your **Orange** Sacral Chakra, up to your **Yellow** Solar Plexus Chakra, up to your Green Heart Chakra, up to your **Blue** Throat Chakra, up to your **Indigo** Spiritual Eye Chakra, up to your **Violet** Crown Chakra. Visualize rainbow sparkles of healing light shooting out the top of your head pulsating throughout your entire energetic fields. Give thanks to Mother Earth for allowing you to ground into her and give thanks to the Light of Father God for helping you to open and clear out your chakras. Slowly return to your normal state of consciousness.

Chakras

The Seven Seals Of God Consciousness

Reclaiming wholeness and divine union with our God self requires us to not only embrace the physical body but also our spiritual or energetic bodies. Our energetic body surrounds and penetrates our physical body with our predominant energy centers or chakras running from the top of our head, down our spine, to the bottom of our feet. Chakra literally means "wheel of light." Chakras are energy vortices that bring energy from the universal life field into our entire human system. Chakras are the regulators of spiritual life force energy, prana or chi. Without properly functioning chakras our health is vulnerable due to a of lack of healthy energy that is able to move through our chakras. In addition, the lack of chi or energy that can be brought into our system will limit the potential for a spiritual opening that leads us into greater states of consciousness.

Through our chakras we send out energies affecting other people and the events in our lives. If a chakra is blocked or distorted the intake of energy will be depleted or excessive not only affecting us but also the people we interact with. Every thought and feeling we have passes through our chakras. When we allow ourselves to fully feel the emotions our thoughts and feelings stir up within us, our chakras will process the energy and allow it to flow through us so it can be released. Oftentimes, we resist negative feelings and emotions and we end up creating restrictions and blocks within our chakras creating imbalance in our system leading to illness. Each chakra is associated with a specific organ in our body. If a chakra is out of balance, it affects the correlating organs creating disharmony and dis-ease. All illness begins in the energy body first before it makes its way to the physical body. Thus, all illness has a spiritual / energetic origin. A healthy human system occurs when all chakras are aligned, balanced and functioning with an open flow.

For meditation purposes we will focus on the seven primary chakras that directly affect our physical body. Our primary chakras are the rainbow bridge that connects our physical body to our Spirit and they are the same colors as a rainbow. Our first chakra is red, our second is orange, our third is yellow, our fourth is green our fifth is blue, our sixth is indigo and our seventh is violet (ROYGBIV). In the Bible, these are also known as the seven seals. Each chakra is a doorway or portal into higher consciousness and once they are understood, opened and cleared we move into a state of wholeness bringing our Spirit down into matter. Our chakras are the bridge that unite Heaven and Earth energies. This balance between Heaven and Earth or Spirit and Matter requires a total surrender to God leading to the activation of the high heart. Once our lower chakras (Earth / Matter / Physicality) are transcended we activate our thymus gland or high heart chakra assisting with the opening of our upper chakras (Heaven / Spirit / Intuition) leading us into a state of heightened spiritual development. Our heart chakra balances the lower chakras helping us to stay grounded on the earth plane while the upper chakras allow us to draw in an expanded amount of divine love and wisdom. Once all chakras are cleared, aligned and balanced our heart chakra will activate the pineal, pituitary and hypothalmus glands signaling the kundalini to rise bringing our divine spirit into matter. When this occurs we merge with our God Self experiencing Divine Love, Unity, Ecstasy and Bliss. In this state, we experience the truth of God, that God is Love. We realize we are connected and never have been separated from God, anyone or anything in the universe. We realize the perfection of every perceived imperfect situation that has occurred in our life and we know that all is in divine order. We enter into a place of Divine Mind and understand greater universal patterns. We understand our reason for being here and develop a strong connection with our God Self, purifying our soul, leading us into our highest soul's potential.

Through meditation, visualization, purification and intention the kundalini will rise in perfect divine timing for each individual creating their own rainbow bridge of light into the higher realms of awareness and enlightenment. This process begins with the clearing and balancing of each chakra and the clearing, balancing and integration of the many layers of the human energetic field. Choosing to clear our chakras and energy fields will lead us into a greater understanding of ourselves and each other. The benefits are well worth it! Even the symbol for Medicine is a Caduceus which is a rod entwined with two serpents (DNA) in the form of a double helix. The rod represents the chakra system that runs along the spine and the double helix or snakes represent the kundalini energy rising up through each chakra opening us up to our God self which will activate our dormant strands of DNA. The Caduceus is a symbol for good health and when our chakras are open and functioning properly and our dormant strands of DNA activated our flow of Spirit (life force energy) will be greatly enhanced. When this occurs our physical bodies will naturally return to a place of health and balance, we will become mentally clear, our emotions will have less control over us and our connection to Spirit will be strengthened. This process is a journey and does require personal commitment, dedication, desire and strong intention to heal. However, this process should not be forced! The raising of energy from the root chakra all the way up the spine to the crown chakra requires patience, trust, faith and *self-purification*. Divine energy will rise at exactly the right time for each soul's journey. Your focused attention on meditation and the clearing of your chakras and energy fields will activate your kundalini to rise when your system has been adequately prepared. Please do not force this process.

Activation of our Rainbow Bridge

The first three chakras (Root, Sacral and Solar Plexus) are our 3rd dimensional chakras and represent our yang, masculine, dark energies. These chakras are very important because they help us manifest and create our desires here on Earth. When they are functioning properly we are fully in our power using it in a balanced, conscious, healthy manner to benefit the **whole** of humanity. We easily manifest our highest soul's potential, we speak our truth and we set healthy boundaries. Unfortunately, many peoples lower three chakras are heavily distorted and unbalanced. That's why our planet reflects chaos, turmoil, illness and separation. These chakras must be purified before we can rise above our ego's defense system, our dualistic natures and our unconscious creations. We cannot fully open and utilize our higher chakras (Heart, Throat, Spiritual Eye and Crown) until our lower ones are cleared, balanced and integrated. If the lower chakras and the higher chakras are not working properly, a true awakening and activation of our divine energy cannot occur. We cannot deny any aspect of ourselves! We each have dark and light and masculine and feminine energy running through our systems. In order to be whole we must integrate and balance ALL aspects of our being.

Root Chakra: The Body of God

The First Dimensional Chakra: (ROOT)

It is associated with the color RED.

The Root chakra is located at the base of the spine. It is very important because it builds the foundation for all of the other chakras. If our root chakra is out of balance, it affects the balance and harmony of every chakra. It is associated with the physical body and grounds us onto the Earth plane. When we are fully grounded, we easily manifest our needs and desires without harming another. Our creations are in divine alignment and created with the purest of intentions. When our root chakra is balanced we have no need or desire to manipulate, force or control another with distorted energy to get what we want.

Balanced Root Chakra: We are grounded and centered. Our physical body is vital and healthy. We are connected to our instincts and we feel safe and supported. We have faith in our own personal manifesting abilities and we do not expect others to take care of us. We do not give our power away and we know we are fully capable of providing all of the basic human necessities needed for our survival. We are a leader, not a follower. We are stable, healthy, courageous, patient and powerful.

Unbalanced Root Chakra: Survival issues. Money issues: over focused on making money even at the expense of others (greed) or the inability to make money in order to provide for your basic necessities. Anger, violence, fear, lack of self worth (leading to self centeredness), disorganization, fearful, restless, anxious, disconnected from the body (overweight / underweight / unhealthy), lack of faith, inability to relax, inability to stay grounded, loosing our center and oftentimes over reacting, inablity to be in the present moment - always in the past or in the future.

Traumas to the Root Chakra: Traumatic Birth, Difficult Childhood, Insufficient Bonding with Mother, Physical Abuse, Abandonment, Fearful Environment, Distorted and Controlling Religious Beliefs.

Bodily Symptoms Expressing Blockage: Constipation, Bone Disorders, Weight Problems, Sciatica, Degenerative Arthritis, Knee Trouble, Eating Disorders, Aging, Gastrointestinal Disorders.

A large portion of our society has a blocked or unbalanced root chakra. The majority of us were raised by well intentioned but unawake parents who were unable to provide us with the nurturing necessary to fully develop this chakra. The root chakra is developed while we are in the womb and up until around 12 months. If we were raised in a safe, loving, nurturing environment the chances of our root chakra developing fully are very high, therefore, providing a very strong foundation for the rest of our chakras to fully develop. If this chakra is not developed our foundation will be shaky and our roots will not be strong enough to provide continued support for our highest growth potential. When this occurs, we protect ourselves by withdrawing our Spirit from fully grounding into our root chakra so we can avoid experiencing our pain. Although this serves a purpose by helping us move through emotional traumatic events in our lives; if we do not eventually re-open the root chakra, allowing the life force energies from the Earth and our Spirit to enter our system, we will become depleted leading to an energetic imbalance, illness and disease.

In addition many religions, governments and the media induce inappropriate levels of fear keeping people stagnated in their root chakra. Fear of God, fear of people with different beliefs, fear of food shortages, viral outbreaks, food contamination, invading countries, nuclear threats and a failing economy keep us stuck in a perpetual state of fear making it very difficult for our root chakra to function properly. In addition, many of us have bought into the belief that we are separate from each other and God and it is our separation consciousness that creates all suffering and fear. When we begin to grasp the idea that we are each divine sparks, NEVER separated from God we will be able to remove the cages of fear that enslave us. Fear is the demon of the root chakra. In order to release our fears we must first admit we have them in order to transform them. Ignorance is not bliss and denial keeps us stuck. Once we acknowledge our fears and work through them they will be released clearing the blocks we have created in our root chakra. Once they are cleared we free up space for earth energy to move into and through our root chakra ascending up into our second chakra called the Sacral Chakra.

Sacral Chakra: The Will of God

Second Dimensional Chakra: (Sacral)

It is associated with the color ORANGE

The Sacral Chakra is located in the lower abdomen below the naval and is developed during the age of 6-24 months. It is associated with procreation, assimilation of food, creativity, sexuality, vitality, desire, the will of spirit and emotional balance. When our sacral chakra is balanced we are willing to feel our emotions and are able to express ourselves without loosing our center. We enjoy pleasurable activities without having the need to overindulge in things that compromise our health and well-being. Unfortunately, many of us were taught not to express our emotions leading to emotional instability and the desire to numb our emotions with food, drugs and alcohol.

In addition, the sacredness and power of our sexual energy has been greatly distorted and abused. Religions create shame, depression and denial of sexuality while big corporations use sex and sexually explicit messages to increase sells. Sex is either denied or overindulged creating all kinds of perversions, and addictions. We have lost touch with the intimacy and sacredness of sexual union partly because we have also shut down our emotional bodies. Unfortunately, blocking the natural flow of emotions and the powerful forces of our sexual energy creates blocks within our system that inhibits our natural flow of life force energy from cleansing and healing our entire system.

Balanced Sacral Chakra: Able to Express Yourself, Emotional Intelligence, Ability to Experience Pleasure, Healthy Sexuality, Nurtures Self and Others, Healthy Boundaries, Open to Change, Works Harmoniously with Others.

Unbalanced Sacral Chakra: Overindulgent in Food, Drugs, Alcohol, Material Things and Sex. Confusion, Lacking Purpose, Thrives in Crisis, Jealousy, Sexual Difficulties, Impotence, Poor Boundaries, Disconnected from Others.

Traumas to the Sacral Chakra: Sexual or Emotional Abuse, Neglect, Denial of Child's Feelings, Alcoholic or Drug Addicted Families, Religious Extremes

Bodily Symptoms Expressing Blockage: Sexual Dysfunction, Impotence, Aging, Stiff Lower Back, Inflexible, Uterine, Bladder or Kidney Problems

The Sacral Chakra is where we process our emotions. Many people are disconnected from their emotions (sacral chakra) because their root chakra is blocked. They are fearful (root) of lovingly and authentically expressing how they truly feel (sacral). Many of us were taught that crying and sharing our emotions was a sign of weakness. We bought into the idea that emotions were bad and ended up doing great harm to our sacral chakra. Instead of feeling our feelings and allowing our emotions to be expressed, in a healthy way, we tend to block them denying that they ever existed.

When we actively begin healing the sacral chakra old stuffed emotions from our past, specifically our childhood, will begin to surface so they can be felt, expressed and finally released. In addition, memories of times you have hurt others will also be revealed for a final clearing. In order to truly heal and clear out our sacral chakra we need to revisit our disowned emotional aspects of ourselves that we have denied. Once these blocks are removed, we will free up space in our sacral chakra for divine energy to move up into our third chakra, the Solar Plexus.

Solar Plexus Chakra: The Hand of God

Third Dimensional Chakra: (Solar Plexus)

It is associated with the color YELLOW

The Solar Plexus is located above the navel and below the chest. It is developed between the ages of 18 months to 4 years old. This chakra is where we hold our self-esteem, power and individuality. It is here where our sympathetic nervous system is vitalized and our metabolism and digestive processes occur. When our solar plexus is balanced we allow our balanced emotions (sacral) to create a positive life experience fully empowered (solar plexus) to create the life of our dreams (root). We are powerful, full of life, supportive and hold all life with a loving embrace.

When this chakra is distorted, the ego is in control. We literally **Edge God Out** by creating blocks within our system keeping our God self energies and highest source of wisdom and knowledge from guiding us. Our egoic, human personality takes over and thinks it's the boss leading to all sorts of distortions greatly affecting everything in our path. Because all of our chakras work together if one is out of balance it will affect the others. If our root and sacral are out of balance then our solar plexus will also be affected creating aggressive behaviors. The need to dominate and control others (solar plexus), greed and war become the norm when we are not grounded and connected to the Earth (root) and we have denied our powerful sexual energies and emotions (sacral). Energy never dies; it is in a constant state of movement. This distorted excessive energy moves through our system putting the solar plexus in overdrive. Peace becomes impossible and an insatiable desire to control others surfaces. Tremendous imbalance occurs between the aggressors and those who have depleted solar plexus energies. People become enslaved in a system dominated by masculine aggressive energies unable to tap into their own innate power creating a viscous cycle of disempowerment and control. That's why our planet reflects chaos, turmoil, illness and separation because our lower chakras are either blocked or overactive keeping us from moving divine energy up into our heart chakra activating the truth of our being.

Balanced Solar Plexus: Divine Will Manifested in Physical Reality, Self-control, Able to Meet Challenges, Responsible, Transformative, Personal Power, Healthy Self Esteem, Warm Personality, Playful and Spontaneous, Humorous, A Leader not a Follower, Able to Speak our Truth and Set Boundaries.

Unbalanced Solar Plexus: Attention on Power and Recognition, Domineering, Angry, Arrogant, Need to be Right, Inability to Slow Down, Competitive, Attracted to Sedatives OR Attracted to Stimulants, Weak Will, Low Energy, Easily Manipulated, Passive.

Traumas to the Solar Plexus: Authoritarianism, Domineering Relationships, Excessive and Unrealistic Responsibilities, Shaming, Physical and Emotional abuse.

Bodily Symptoms Expressing Blockage: Digestive Disorders, Ulcers, Blood Sugar Problems, Chronic Fatigue, Hypertension, Liver Problems, Gall Bladder Problems

Many of us use our power incorrectly. We are either powerless and don't believe in ourselves or we use our power to dominate and control others. Oftentimes, we give our power away to families, friends, churches, governments, and doctors because we don't want to accept responsibility for ourselves and make the changes necessary to transcend everything holding us back from reaching our highest soul's potential. We falsely believe it is easier to allow others to figure everything out for us, telling us what to do, rather than relying on our own abilities and intuitive wisdom from our inner being. Giving our power away or desiring to control others is detrimental to our solar plexus chakra.

Many people blocked in this chakra have bought into the belief that they are separate from God and are helpless victims of their circumstances. They block energy from flowing freely keeping them from aligning with their divine self, the true source of their power. They don't realize they are the creators of their reality and have the power to choose at anytime to make different choices to create a better life for themselves. This creates anger and frustration blocking divine energy from moving up into the fourth chakra, the Heart Chakra.

Heart Chakra: The Heart of God

Fourth Dimensional Chakra: (Heart):

It is associated with the color GREEN.

The heart chakra is located in the chest and is developed between the ages of 4-7 years. When the heart chakra is opened it holds the energy of Peace, Compassion, Unconditional Love, Honesty and Harmony. These energies cannot be fully felt, understood and integrated until the lower and higher chakras are cleared, balanced and activated. The heart chakra is the place of balance between our lower, masculine, dark (human ego) and our higher, feminine, light (God) selves. Our heart chakra is the entryway to our soul and it cannot be fully opened until we integrate the light and dark within us. We each need to accept and understand our dualistic / human / egoic / divine natures in order to reach a place of non-duality and transformation. It is in our heart chakra where we learn to embrace and love our vulnerabilities, darkness, limitations, hurt and pain so we can transcend the smallness of our human ego and grow towards something greater and more expansive. Our heart is our center, our essence, our spiritual core. Once the heart chakra is fully activated, it will awaken our soul consciousness and the higher chakras bringing our Spirit down into our physical being. Our heart and soul is the bridge to the God Mind where we end duality of matter and Spirit unifying ourselves into a place of connection, wholeness and inner peace. When the heart is fully opened we remember our divinity and allow the love of creation to flow through us. We remember that we are God in human form and this recognition of the self also helps us to recognize the divinity in everyone and everything else. In this state, we recognize the interconnectedness in everything!

The heart chakra is the integration point between the upper (light) and lower (dark) chakras; it is the center of our human cross or physical body. Every time we block a chakra we crucify ourselves, keeping us from fully accessing our highest soul's potential and union with our God self. Because all humans have experienced many lifetimes where love has been withheld, we have an epidemic of wounded hearts that need to be healed. Because of this, we have created energetic shields over our hearts to protect ourselves. We shut down our emotional bodies disconnecting us from our heart centered consciousness and intuition allowing our egoic minds to take over. We closed our hearts and blocked the continuous flow of love from the ecstatic presence of our God self.

Until the heart chakra is fully opened we will not be able to flow divine energy into our high heart or thymus gland where our divine spark is ignited and our Christ Consciousness is expanded. The "Return of Christ" is the activation of each individuals Christ Consciousness which activates our Christed Luminous Light Body. When this occurs to every person on the planet we will literally create Heaven here on Earth. We are all Christed, regardless of what religion, or lack of religion we choose to follow. It is our divine birthright and we all carry the Christ Seed within our being. Once our lower and higher chakras are cleared our divine heart will be activated releasing the need to crucify ourselves or another and we will no longer need to carry the burden of our human egoic cross that creates suffering.

Balanced Heart Chakra: Oneness with Life, Healing, True Forgiveness, Courage, Honesty, Healthy Relationships, Healthy Boundaries, Balance, Unconditional Love, Faith, Peace, Compassion, Harmony, Openness, Balance of Giving and Receiving, Emotional Wisdom, Joy, Bliss, Expansion, Self Preservation, Self Love, Self Nurturance.

Unbalanced Heart Chakra: Withholding Love, Separation, Controlling, Demanding, Antisocial, Critical, Judgmental, Depression, Lack of Empathy, Lack of Boundaries, Codependent, Jealousy, Conditional Love

Traumas To the Heart Chakra: Rejection, Abandonment, Betrayal, Physical and Emotional Abuse, Grief, Sexual Abuse, Death of a Loved One, Divorce

Bodily Symptoms Expressing Blockage: Heart Disorders, Circulatory Dysfunction, Lung Disorders, Tension between Shoulders, Weak Immune System.

Many of us have endured difficult soul lessons in this lifetime due to our soul's desire to clear and heal its residual karma and distorted energy from all previous lifetimes. Because of this, many of us have experienced great pain and disharmony. Once we understand that pain can be used as a catalyst for transformation and every experience that has ever happened to us was created by us for greater soul growth, then we can fully step into a place of complete surrender, acceptance and forgiveness. When we allow our hearts to fully open we create a bridge between our lower chakras and our higher chakras fully stepping into our power becoming heart centered conscious creators of our circumstances. We will no longer need to suffer the consequences of our unconscious creations. Once the heart chakra is cleared and opened, divine energy will continue to move up into the fifth chakra called the Throat Chakra.

Throat Chakra: The Voice of God

Fifth Dimensional Chakra: (Throat):

It is associated with the color Blue.

The throat chakra holds the energy of communication. It is located in the area between the shoulders and the neck and is developed during the ages of 7-12 years. Not only is the throat chakra used for communication between people but it is also how God and our higher self speaks through us from the higher realms. If this chakra is not functioning properly, not only will our communication with others be difficult but we will also not be receiving clear guidance from our divine self, oftentimes leading us down a difficult path and a hard lesson to learn from. Although there are no mistakes, or wrong paths there are choices that we make that sometimes are not in the highest good for all involved. There are consequences for every choice and there are always lessons to be learned from our lower self choices that are not guided by our higher selves. When our throat chakra is fully opened we will be guided by truth from the higher realms and from our divine essence. We will no longer need to be guided by other people, belief systems, laws or anything that limits us from living our highest potential because we will be fully expressing our divinity in all things we do.

Unfortunately, many of our throat chakras are closed because we live in fear of speaking our truth. We don't want to voice our feelings and we certainly don't want to verbalize any kind of information that may provide a different perspective or perhaps go against the already ingrained belief systems of the mass consciousness. In previous lifetimes many of us have been burnt, beaten, imprisoned, rejected, ridiculed and even crucified for speaking our truth and trying to empower our brothers and sisters. Unfortunately, these deeply seated fears of speaking up need to be overcome and we need to be willing to express our divinity and truth without preaching. When we truly remember who we are, our self-image will be reestablished and we will be equipped with the courage and discernment to know how to properly express the energies of our voice with words of love and compassion.

Balanced Throat Chakra: Clear, Truthful Communication, Authentic, Balanced, Grounded Relationships, Able To Express Feelings Through Words, Good Listener, Expresses Creativity, Open to Guidance from Higher Sources

Unbalanced Throat Chakra: Lies, Fearful Of Speaking The Truth, Lack of Communication or Excessive Talking, Gossiping, Guided by the Ego, Unable To Receive Clear Guidance From The Higher Realms.

Traumas to the Throat Chakra: Verbal Abuse, Constant Yelling, Families With Addictions, Excessive Criticism, Refusing to Speak, Domination and Control.

Bodily Symptoms Expressing Blockage: Toxic Body, Ear, Nose and Throat Problems, Jaw Problems (TMJ), Thyroid

Communication is the connecting principle that makes life possible. Without communication, nothing can survive. Everything in the Universe is in a constant state of communication. When communication is blocked or ceases to exist, healthy relationship is no longer sustained. In order to survive, the human body must be in a constant state of communication with itself. The heart communicates with the blood, hormones communicate with the cells and brain waves communicate with our muscles and tissues. Communication is the essence of life! Without communication there is no relationship!

Once the lower chakras are cleared and divine energy activates the heart, we begin to transcend our lower, darker chakras and move into the higher, lighter chakras connecting us with our divinity and our God Self. We begin to move out of limitation, boundaries and separation into an understanding of deep inter-connectedness with God and all living things. When the throat chakra is fully opened, balanced and functioning properly it becomes a gateway to the higher planes of the Spiritual realms. Clear communication between God, your higher self, angels and spirit guides becomes possible. It is here where we begin to transcend the confinements of the physical body and are able to tap into the multidimensional depths of our mind and Spirit. We become conscious creators of our life experience and begin to "hear" the thoughts running through our mind that create our reality. Instead of being a victim of our thoughts, we step into an empowered position where we are able to quickly clear negative thinking by replacing it with positive affirmations and intentions. Once the throat chakra is opened, our vibration is raised and we begin to understand that everything is energy including our thoughts and words. Vibrationally, we will begin to resonate with like-minded people, events, activities and beliefs that reflect the vibrational frequency of an open throat chakra.

We will desire and attract positive, truthful, authentic, grounded, open, honest communication in all areas of our life. Once the energies of the throat chakra are cleared, space will be created for divine energy to flow up from the throat chakra into the sixth chakra the Brow or Spiritual Eye Chakra.

May those who have eyes, see; and those who have ears, hear.
Matthew 13: 9-17

Spiritual Eye Chakra: The Eye of God
Sixth Dimensional Chakra: (Brow / Third Eye Chakra)
It is associated with the color Indigo (dark blue).

The Brow or Third Eye chakra carries the energy of Clear Seeing and Discernment. It is located in the center of the head in between the physical eyes. This chakra opens the door to our multidimensional senses helping us to move away from the dense limitations of an egoic, materialistic, physical world based on illusion. Once our spiritual eye begins to open, deeper spiritual truths will resonate with us and the veil of illusion will begin to deteriorate. An open spiritual eye reveals the truth of reality. Without it, empowered spiritual discernment is not possible!

A large portion of the planet has a blocked Brow Chakra. Humanity is very materialistic and is focused strictly on the physical world and what the physical world can provide for them. Because their spiritual eye is closed, people are unable to recognize their divinity. They fall into the egos trap of lack and disempowerment and try to fill their void with material gains, at the expense of others, while their soul is desperate for the spiritual wealth and nourishment only their God self can provide.

Most of Humanity only believes what they see with their physical eyes totally disregarding the spiritual realms. In truth, we don't even see with our physical eyes, we see with our mind. Science, religion and education have stifled our imaginations. We have placed ourselves, God and everything else in a tight, neat little box literally blocking the energies of our higher, intuitive senses. When this occurs, truth and discernment cannot be fully accessed. Therefore, we are easily misled, tricked and lied to. Restrictions in the energies of this chakra keep us from being able to get to the "root" of our problems, create irrational fears and keep us in a state of disconnection and separation from others.

Balanced Brow Chakra: Soul Realization, Spiritual Awareness, Intuition, Clairvoyance, Imagination, Discernment, Able to Visualize, Able to Manifest, Good Memory, Divine Mind, Wisdom, Inner Knowingness, Perception beyond Duality, Multidimensional Sensory System, Higher Psychic Senses, Sixth Sense, Truth, Vision.

Unbalanced Brow Chakra: Denial, Obsessions, Lack of Imagination, Poor Memory, Insensitive, Hallucinations, Cynical, Overly Detached from the World, Irrational Fears, Lack of Discernment, Illusion, Stuck in 3D, Limited view of Reality.

Trauma to the Brow Chakra: Invalidation of Intuition and Psychic Experiences, Living in a Fear Filled Environment, Rigid / Fear Filled Thought and Belief Systems.

Bodily Symptoms Expressing Blockage: Tension, Headaches, Eye Problems, Ear Nose Throat Disorders, Blockage of Physical and Multidimensional Senses: Touch, Taste, Sight, Hearing and Smell

The third eye chakra is related to the pineal gland, the Seat of the Soul. When it is activated, light coded information from each individuals higher intelligence is downloaded awakening the super conscious mind. Deeper spiritual truths are attained, consciousness is expanded and the ability to overcome the human ego becomes possible. It is the ego that creates the veil between Spirit and man creating spiritual blindness. This veil keeps people from being able to perceive the higher planes of existence and wisdom keeping them in the illusion of the third dimension. Opening of the spiritual eye helps people to "see" the patterns, limited beliefs and limited thinking that needs to be transcended in order to advance the soul.

How open and allowing we are, will determine the openness of our spiritual eye. It does not have to be fully open in order for us to begin to access spiritual truth and spiritual discernment. If you have made it this far in the book without discarding it, your spiritual eye is already somewhat opened. When it is fully opened and attuned we are able to see and communicate with angels, spirit guides and the ascended masters. The limitations of time and space are transcended and precognition and remote viewing become possible. All of these abilities are our divine birthright. Multidimensional hearing, seeing, feeling and touching can be achieved by anyone willing to develop their higher senses. Did you know your

Soul has it's own unique scent, sound, color and vibration unlike any other being in creation! Some highly attuned souls are actually able to tap into that part of your being. Once we all open ourselves up to our higher senses, advanced powers of discernment will be available and no one will be able to lie to us again.

Unfortunately, religion and the belief in the wrath of God creates a tremendous amount of fear in people keeping them from accessing their already innately divine gifts. In order to open your spiritual eye you will need to integrate your fears and have a strong desire to break free from the illusions you have bought into. Each of us are incredibly expansive multidimensional beings always connected to God. The greatest illusion we have ever bought into is the concept of separation from God and each other. Once we fully understand and trust that God is Love and is always with us, our fears will begin to unravel. Facing our fears and allowing the spiritual eye to open will allow divine energy to flow up into the seventh chakra called the Crown Chakra. Once this occurs, Empowerment, Divine Illumination, God Realization, Oneness, Unity and Bliss become our reality.

Crown Chakra: Thousand Petal Lotus of Spirit
Seventh Dimensional Chakra: (Crown):
It is associated with the color Violet, Gold and White

The Crown Chakra carries the energies of Enlightenment, Divine Illumination and God Realization. It is located on the top of the head and is the source of our higher consciousness. When fully opened, the Crown Chakra becomes the conduit through which our Holy Spirit, God Self, Christed Self, Buddhic Self or Divine Essence is brought down into our physical being. When all seven of the chakras are opened and aligned and we have purified ourselves and have become totally harmless, the "Gifts of the Holy Spirit" are returned to us. (1 Corinthians 12)

Balanced Crown Chakra: Wisdom, Mastery, Unification of the God Self with Human Personality, Bliss, Intuition, Expanded Consciousness, Knowingness, Transcendence, Oneness, Deep Understanding, Service to Others, Spiritual Energy

Unbalanced Crown Chakra: Confusion, Lack of Understanding, Insensitive, Lack of Inspiration, Apathy, Greed, Overly Rational and Materialistic, Domination of Others, Spiritual Cynicism, Addiction, Attachment, Over Intellectualization, Disassociation to the Physical Body, God, Humanity, the Earth and the Animals, Desensitization to the Realms of Spirit

Trauma to the Crown Chakra: Forced Religion and Blind Obedience

Bodily Symptoms Expressing Blockage: Migraines, Inability to Focus / Confusion, Deterioration of the Central Nervous System, Emotional Depression, Desensitization, Lack of Feeling, Accelerated Aging / Deterioration of the Physical Body.

The Crown Chakra is often called the thousand petal lotus. Throughout history it has been depicted in paintings of Jesus the Christ, Buddha, Saints, Angels and other highly evolved beings as a golden white halo around their heads. When the Crown Chakra is fully opened an awareness of our divinity and the true essence of our being is understood and integrated. The crown chakra will not fully open until all seven of the chakras and corresponding energy fields have been purified enough for divine energy to be released activating the Kundalini. The Kundalini is a divine spiral of energy similar to a coiled snake that lays dormant at the base of each person's spine (root chakra) until proper purification has occurred within a beings system for it to safely ascend up the chakra column. The crown chakra connects us to our masculine Father God while the root chakra connects us to our feminine Mother Goddess or Mother Earth. If the kundalini is able to move through each chakra and does not encounter any blocks it will move up into the crown chakra opening a pathway for each persons God self to descend into their physical body. Kundalini is Creator energy. It is our divine birthright to activate this part of ourselves so we can become conscious co-creators here on Earth. When our system is properly prepared, the descension of our God self washes over each of the seven chakras breaking the seven seals activating the creation of our divine luminous light body. This prepares us to move forward into Self Mastery where we have the *potential* to fully activate and embody our Holy Grail becoming a Divine Enlightened Human.

Mastery and the Activation of the Holy Grail

The Holy Grail is the merging of our God Self / Spirit / Holy Ghost with our Soul bringing it down into the physical body or the temple of the Grail. It is the activation and empowerment of the Christ consciousness. The physical body (temple of the Grail) and the emotional and mental bodies (Soul) must be prepared and purified before the soul body can be infused with Spirit (Holy Ghost). Each of our seven chakras (Seven Seals) must be cleared, aligned and balanced before the activation of the Holy Grail can begin. The seven seals represent the seven levels of mans development and what we must transform and purify so we can become a divine being of light. Each of us, must choose for ourselves, to climb the mountain of self (Rising to the Mount of Spirit) for our own personal transfiguration to occur.

Dedication to our spiritual growth and active involvement in our personal transformation is absolutely necessary. We need to integrate all of the parts of ourselves, perfect our personality, purify our chakras and energy fields, raise our vibration and prepare our body to fully express the illumination of our souls infused with our Divine Spirit. Each of us will be required to rise above our egos defense system, the false image of self, and step into the truth and integrity of our God essence. This process can be very intense, that's why most people avoid it all together spending lifetimes repeating the same karmic cycles because they refuse to step onto the path of spiritual transformation and enlightenment. When we choose to truly align ourselves with God our spiritual self will merge with our physical being breaking the seven seals that have been placed over our chakras opening us up for a deeper level of soul purification. Spiritual lessons and initiations will be intensified and situations and events will be "set-up" by our God self and Master Guides to further our soul's development. During this process, our God self will illuminate our magnificence, as well as, the shadowy rejected parts of ourselves that need to be healed and integrated. We will no longer be able to hide in the shadows of our unresolved psychology or egoic personality. We will be required to look ourselves in the mirror with brutal self-honesty and take responsibility for all of the rejected parts of ourselves that are demanding our attention. Our God self, will lovingly show us what needs to be transformed and usually it will be through observation of another person's behavior reflecting back to us the very thing that needs to be transformed in our own being. Be aware that the ego can play tricks on us at any stage of awakening and throw us back into the world of illusion. **No one is exempt from the tricks of the ego!** Our lower selves or ego can not be truly transformed until the light of our God self has merged with us in order to provide us with the spiritual support necessary to further enhance the clean up of our soul. A strong connection to our God self will help us stay in a receptive state, fully aligned with the divine, helping us to acknowledge those aspects of ourselves that need to be healed without getting consumed in judgment and blame. Our God self will help us stay in alignment assisting us in the knowingness that there is a bigger plan, a greater healing and something much larger at play here that we may not be fully aware of. Connection with our God self lovingly helps us embrace the process guiding us through difficult soul lessons leading us into a greater sense of wholeness, mastery and beauty.

It is helpful to remain humble and truthful with ourselves about what is happening so we can quickly pull ourselves out of the egos trick of victim consciousness and back into self-empowerment. We will need to view every difficult soul interaction as an opportunity to learn at an even deeper level than before. Everything that has ever occurred in our lives, or will occur, is a learning experience that prepares us to receive the Holy Grail. The closer we get, the deeper the purification! Stepping into surrender and allowance and keeping our hearts open through forgiveness and love will assist us in moving through our difficult soul lessons more quickly so we can activate the grail of wisdom and the light of divinity within our being. When difficult soul interactions arise, we need to ask ourselves: What is my Spirit trying to communicate to me through this person's behavior? What fear is this person demonstrating that is a reflection of my own? What part of my psychology made me vulnerable to this person or situation? What is the hidden lesson? Conscious, active, self-evaluation is the key to our transformation. Blame and judgment are warning signs that we have fallen off the inner path of self-transcendence and have stepped onto the outer path of ego resistance. The true path of salvation, self-transcendence and personal Christhood can only be found on the inner path. Everything happens for a reason and there is always a hidden lesson for both souls behind every interaction. If we don't learn from our experiences we will attract another one to learn from. Keep in mind that everything always goes back to the self. Everything that occurs in our life is always an outer projection of our own inner workings or a lesson we have brought to ourselves for the growth of our soul. Everything that needs to be healed will be brought to the surface to be transformed! If we refuse to face these unhealed aspects of ourselves an escalation of crisis and difficulty will occur. What we resist, persist! Our Spirit is giving us a warning sign that something within our being is feeling neglected and is being disowned. By acknowledging our unhealed aspects and welcoming them back into our being we can integrate the wisdom they are trying to show us transforming ourselves into a deeper state of wholeness. Once our God self has merged with our physical being and has taken dominion over our lower self or ego we will no longer be blinded by the veil of illusion. Our consciousness will be expanded, we will be healed on many levels of our being, we will recognize self created patterns that need to be transformed and we will be lovingly guided by our divine essence moving us forward into Mastery and the activation and integration of our Holy Grail.

The Holy Grail is the Divine Enlightened Human with an activated chakra system creating a "rainbow bridge" between Heaven and Earth. The physical self (here on Earth) unites with the God self (in a higher octave or Heaven) and creates a bridge between the physical and spiritual worlds. Our physical body's vibration must be raised, as well as, our consciousness expanded in order for the descension of Spirit (Holy Ghost) to occur. The merging of our Holy Spirit with matter cannot be attained until the human personality or ego and the physical body has risen its vibration high enough for Divine union to occur. Once union has occurred, our entire system becomes a vessel of divine light, a container, a cup or a chalice in which the light of Creator freely pours into our being activating our Holy Grail. The purified Divine Human is the Holy Grail and once it is activated within a being they become "containers of light" here on Earth that interact with the energy fields of other souls activating them so their systems can be prepared for Divine Union as well. This is God's desire for everyone on Earth. However, it is a choice we must make for ourselves, God will not make the decision for us. Once our Holy Grail has been activated, we will learn to be in the world but not of it closing the gap of perceived separation between God and the entire diversity of creation. The ultimate goal of every soul on the planet is to rise above the limitations of duality and separation remembering who we are so we can become conscious co-creators and activate our highest Divine potential. This is the soul's ultimate mission! Each of us can truly bring our own HEAVEN HERE DOWN ON EARTH. We are Divine Beings, direct extensions of God and this is the Divine Plan!

Today, more than ever, the potential for spiritual awakening and soul growth for every human is accelerated as we approach the center of the galaxy. The love coming from the central sun, the cosmic rays of light and the heightened energies of the Christ from the photon belt are transforming the consciences and hearts of those who are willing to receive the love, unity and consciousness of "ONE" in their lives. Each of us have total free will as to what we choose to believe and create in our lives. We can choose as many lifetimes as we need to learn and grow and experience the consciousness of polarity and separation or we can choose to advance our souls and move into the light of unification by activating and integrating the Christ Consciousness within our being. Our world is currently split with those choosing to hold onto and remain stuck in the old energy of the collective mind and those choosing to let go of their old beliefs stepping into the new energy of awakening, self-empowerment and mastery. As the Christ energies continue to transform this planet ushering in unity, those choosing to stay in the consciousness of separation and the lower vibrational energies of fear will find themselves behaving chaotically and irrationally. Violence and aggressive defense are the result of humanity buying into the concept that we are separated from God, the Earth and each other. When we believe we are separated, we feel powerless which creates a tremendous amount of fear / darkness within our being. We can choose at anytime to surrender and step into the light of transformation or we can choose to resist the process creating further discord and disharmony in our lives. It is in our hands how we will choose to experience this global transformation, we are not passengers in this process, each of us are responsible for our own ascension!

In order for each of us to make this transition smoothly, we will need to "awaken" our consciousness to the vibration of our soul and the Christ Seed within our hearts. The Christ Seed is the Presence of Christ that dwells within in us and *it must be activated*! For a millennia, humanity as a collective, has chosen to experience life in polarity and separation unaware of the Unity and the Presence of God in everything that exists. We were born asleep, but it is time for us to awaken and activate our highest divine potential! Each of us are divinely sacred beings and it is time that we value our existence and intend to be the change we want for the world. It is time for us to embrace our divine power and become human Christs! We are not limited in any aspect of our power as co-creators. We are at the forefront of this shift and everything is based on the work we have done to prepare us for this global transformation. We are in control of this process and each of us plays an important role in creating Heaven here on Earth. We are an integral part of our ascension journey.

The second coming of Christ manifests through us! When Jesus the Christ incarnated on this planet he seeded all of humanity with the potential to activate our Christ Consciousness. Christ said, "All that I have done, You can do and even greater". We are one with Christ, Source energy and each other. We are all one. We are equal. What one man does all can do, our abilities are based on our **choices**! The real message of Christ is that we are equal to him. We are all sons and daughters of God with the same potentials and abilities. We receive Christ through faith! We receive Christ through our *faith in ourselves* as worthy divine beings who can choose to be the bearers of the Christ Light. "Behold, I stand at the door and knock; if anyone hears my voice, and opens the door, **I will come into him**. (Revelations 3:20) The majority of humanity believes they have already received Christ within their being, but their door (the seven seals / seven chakras / seven energetic portals) have not been purified and opened for their Christ Self to merge with their physical being. Fear, distorted beliefs and the turning away from Self keeps these doors shut! We must go deeply within the Self, into our sacred space, into our hearts through meditation and communion with our masculine, feminine and inner Christ energies before a balancing within our system can occur. This is not an intellectual or emotional experience, it is an incredibly blissful / energetic / spiritual experience which activates our Christ Seed energies merging our Spiritual Self / Christ Self / God Self with our physical being. When this occurs we experience the truth of who we really are. We discover a hidden secret..... that deep inside each of us is the dimension of God and we have *never* been separated from our Creator. "Behold, the kingdom of God is within you, in my Fathers house is many mansions (dimensions). " We discover we are a part God, we are pure love, pure consciousness, free and untethered from the current world we live in. We discover the illusion of this reality, a deeper meaning to our lives and our eternalness. We become one with the Universe and all living things experiencing our contribution to the infinite sea of creation that would not be the same without us. As our Holy Spirit and the Christ Consciousness descend upon us, the fears of our mind and the world completely disappear as we are fully engulfed with the presence of God's love. We have been touched by God's grace and received Christ experiencing a new birth guiding our soul's into their highest expression.

Suggestions for Raising Your Vibration

All who choose to raise their vibration, will be activated! Once you have decided to ascend (raise your frequency) your highest guides, angels and your Spiritual Self and God will begin working with you to help prepare your system for your highest soul's potential. Once your system has been properly prepared, your Christ Seed will be activated! Your INTENTION, your active participation in the clearing of your chakra / energy fields, the expansion of your consciousness and the raising of the physical body's vibration is all that is required of you. Have faith in yourself and the Universe trusting that everything that needs to be shown to you will be shown, everything that needs to be cleared and released will be and everything that needs to be provided will be provided. Everything is in divine order and each of us are lovingly guided and cared for!

Below are several additional suggestions that will help you move through this process with ease and grace. Pick and choose which resonate with you. These are merely suggestions:

1. Celebrate your transition! Each of us are entering into our divine birthright and becoming our Christ Selves! Surrender to this process and allow the truth of your being to be born.

2. Meditate, Meditate, Meditate! **Meditation is the key to spiritual growth; it brings your Spirit down into your physical body.** Prayer is talking to God; meditation is receiving God! Meditation raises your vibration, opens and aligns your chakras, clears out discordant energy from your energy fields, reduces stress, brings you into balance, heals you emotionally, mentally, physically and spiritually. It is also the only way for you to enter sacred space with your Spiritual Self. Ten to Fifteen minutes a day is all that is required.

3. Allow yourself to receive enough rest. During sleep each of us needs to reach a state of relaxation to move into deep RIM so our astral body can lift out of our physical body replenishing our life force energy. This is why we sleep; to rejuvenate our entire energetic and physical system.

4. Energy Work: Energy healers have already awakened and continue to awaken to their divine mission. Find one in your area! They are purposefully spread all over the Earth to assist humanity in the clearing of their energy fields. They are invaluable! They can clear lifetimes of repressed trauma and karma that is creating suffering, pain and imbalance in the human body. Use your discernment and find one you resonate with. Energy healers have gone through a deep healing process themselves allowing their system to be purified enough so they can sustain very high vibrational healing energies of God to flow through them. With the help of God, they can remove large amounts of discordant energy out of your energy field much faster than you doing it all by yourself. Find a DNA Theta Healer!

5. Receive an energetic attunement from an energy healer. An attunement is far more powerful than a healing session. An attunement is a sacred initiation activating **you** to channel an increased level of universal life force energies. When you receive an attunement, your vibration is raised and your energetic system is cleared opening you up to channel higher levels of healing energy. An attunement is a very deep level healing that will connect you more strongly to your Spiritual Self and clear out karmic energy that is ready to be released. An attunement greatly purifies your system so you too can be a strong conduit for God's healing energies helping you to heal yourself, your family, friends, pets and the Earth.

6. Receive a Deeksha / Oneness Blessing. Deeksha is an energy transference that creates neurobiological changes in the brain facilitating personal and global transformation. It balances the left and right sides of the brain which will help move you out of separation and duality consciousness helping you to connect with higher frequencies.

7. Sun bathe! The sun clears out energetic mucous and blocks from our energy field. A lot of us get depressed in the winter because we get less sun building up a toxic residue of mucous. The sun also carries the 5th dimensional energies we need for our transformation, the activation of our DNA and an expansion in our consciousness.

8. Get regular massages. Our muscles contain traumatic cellular memory from our past. Massage helps us to release these memories and helps our body release toxins that keep us from accessing higher vibrations. Look for a massage therapist that is also attuned to the healing energies of Reiki.

9. Get regular exercise! Movement helps clear energetic blocks held within the energy field and helps keep the body and the organs in good working condition. Our organs are working extra hard during this time as we integrate higher energies, it is important to keep them in good working condition. Walking, Yoga, Pilates, Qigong, Tai Chi, Dancing…anything that gets the body moving releases energetic blocks.

10. Detox the body: herbal cleanses for the kidneys, liver or total body. Heavy metal cleanses, parasite cleanses, steam rooms, saunas, epsom salt baths, foot detox baths, energy work, massage, yoga, juice cleanses, fasting, lots of pure drinking water etc…Our physical bodies vibration must be raised and prepared for the descension of Spirit. Visit your local health food store.

11. Become conscious of the foods you eat. Eliminate as many chemicals and processed foods as possible. These foods are dead and are full of toxins. Eat as many water-filled, living "life force" filled foods as possible….. Organic fruits, vegetables, seeds, nuts, grains, fish and poultry. Aim for a PH balanced diet. Avoid the microwave….it radiates (chemotherapies) your food and kills all life force, as well as, fills your home with harmful electromagnetic radiation. Focus on home cooked, **real** food. Visit your local health food store.

12. Become aware of everything you put on your body. Soaps, lotions, bath gels, perfumes, make-up, toothpaste, deodorant, laundry detergents, dish detergents etc….all leave a toxic residue on your skin and enter the bloodstream. Incorporate as many natural products as possible. Visit your local health food store.

13. Drink as much filtered, unfluoridated water as possible. Fluoride can impede our spiritual growth. When our body receives too much fluoride it creates a calcified shield over our pituitary and pineal glands. These are master glands that need to be activated in order for us to merge with our Spiritual Self. Limit caffeine, alcohol and chemical laden sodas, sports drinks etc…from your diet. The body needs spiritually blessed, pure water to transform our dense lower vibrating carbon based cells into higher vibrating crystalline "light filled" cells. Bless your water by placing your hands over it, visualizing it being filled with light and say a small prayer. Ask for the water to be raised in vibration and for the water to be infused with God's healing energy helping your body to release all toxins that are ready to be released.

14. Consciously choose to maintain a pure emotional and mental state at all times. We must become the master of our emotions and thoughts. Our emotional body and mental / intellectual body will misguide us every time. Intuition of the soul speaks through the feelings of our heart, not through our intellect or through our reactive emotions. True inner understanding and knowingness must come from beyond the intellect. It must come from a higher part of our being.

15. Every second of the day provides us with an opportunity to lower or raise our vibrations. Everything is based on the choices we choose to make and our choices reflect our current level of vibration.

16. Be open to releasing those things that no longer serve your highest good. Bless them and release them with love knowing that they have served their purpose. These things may be: old outdated distorted beliefs, low vibrational habits, addictions & activities, high stress / fast paced lifestyle, co-dependant toxic relationships that have had their time, jobs that no longer fulfill your soul.

17. Choose to focus more on your spiritual wealth than your material wealth. Our "stuff" is not eternal but our Spirit is. True power, security and abundance comes from spiritual connection not through money, material goods, prestige, job titles or intellect. We all need to make money to survive in this world but not at the expense of our Soul and Spirit!

18. Step into "surrender" and "acceptance". Our beliefs and behaviors that no longer serve our soul's highest good will need to be released. Our deepest fears, beliefs in limitation and old pain patterns will be brought to the surface through events / set ups / situations that will trigger our awareness so we can consciously acknowledge, resolve and heal them.

19. Choose to release your fears! During this time of acceleration, each of us are re-experiencing lifetimes of deeply ingrained fears. Be kind to yourself as this is a very intense process. Simply remember who you are, a divine extension of God always connected and always guided. Acknowledge your fears; tell your fears they are based in illusion and then release them to the light.

20. Allow yourself to release all of your outdated beliefs that no longer serve your highest good. The majority of our negative beliefs are created from our human ego and are the source of all of our problems. Open yourself up to "knowingness" by taking the time to connect with your God self in your sacred space of meditation. If you do not take the time to connect with your God self you will always be led by the belief systems of other people. Meditate, get connected, experience the peace of "knowingness". Truth can only be found within yourself, allow it to set you free!

21. We need to stay focused on our own inner work. The ego loves to distract us by getting us to focus on everyone else's "stuff". This is a sure fire sign that we have stepped off of the inner path and onto the outer path. The ego blinds us from being able to see the things we need to heal within ourselves. The inner path is the only way to salvation.

22. Stay grounded and centered! As we integrate the higher frequencies we will need to be proactive in keeping ourselves grounded in our body fully present in the NOW moment. Visualize yourself growing energetic roots deep into the Earth every morning when you get out of bed. Exercise, bring your consciousness into the present moment, eat grounding foods and connect with nature and the Earth on a regular basis.

23. In order to ascend we must first descend. Raising our vibrations requires us to tidy up our unfinished business, stuffed emotions, distorted beliefs, disempowering limitations and traumas. We must release the suppressed energy and integrate our incompletions so we can rise up (ascend) to the realm of Spirit bringing our God self (descension) into our being. The ascension path is not a straight shot up, it is more like a roller coaster, descending and ascending until we reach our highest soul's potential.

24. Allow yourself to go through a spiritual detox. Allow all of your negativity, fear, darkness, ego, shadow consciousness, resistance, blame, victim consciousness etc… rise to the surface. Acknowledge it, accept responsibility for it, release the pain of it but keep the wisdom! This is alchemy….turning our darkness into gold.

25. Surround yourself with people who have opened and activated their seven seals bringing their God self down into their body. We are all one, energetically connected, so those who are already activated will enable others, through the principle of resonance, to activate their own inner potential and divine inheritance towards Ascension.

26. Clear your space! As humanity moves through the process of ascension we are sloughing off volumes of accumulated psychic and emotional energy from our accumulated lifetimes. It is very important for us to maintain a sacred space in our homes by keeping them energetically clear. Here are a few suggestions:

- Open the blinds and windows allowing more sun and fresh air to purify your environment. Sun (light) transmutes everything.

- Declutter your home! Low vibrational energies accumulate around our junk!

- During our sleep we process through a lot of our karma and energetic blocks that need to be released. Sometimes this will leave an energetic residue on our sheets. Salt naturally absorbs negative energies. Wash your sheets in ½ C of epsom salt, ½ cup baking soda and a natural laundry detergent. You will sleep better!

- Burn sage, incense or essential oils to purify your environment.

- Play high vibrational music, chimes, bells or drums. Sound carries a vibration and will vibrate stagnant energies away.

- Make your home a safe energetic environment for the whole family. Chaos, turmoil, fighting, yelling, alcohol and drug addictions and low vibrational activities attract low vibrational energies. Like energy attracts like energy! Set your intention to maintain a peaceful, loving, healthy, high vibrational sacred space for your family to live in.

- Intend and visualize your entire space being filled up with the white light of the Holy Spirit. Ask and intend for all discordant energies to be transmuted into their highest expression.

Transmutational / Ascension Symptoms

Ascension is the raising of our personal energy frequency. It occurs when we bring our layers of "light" from our Spiritual Body or Multidimensional God Self down into our physical form. As we integrate more of our true spiritual essence into our being we expand our auric field, chakra system and activate our dormant strands of DNA. This allows us to move into higher states of consciousness accessing a new reality or dimension within ourselves. Please understand when I say higher level of consciousness I do not mean "better". Greater consciousness is "more" consciousness and each one of us has the exact same potential to activate and tap into our higher states of consciousness. Greater consciousness means greater connection to our God Selves and a deeper understanding of the universe. Ascension and the raising of our vibration is a personal spiritual choice. Each of us has the very same potential to ascend; it is a matter of our own free will choice and the intention to allow ourselves to do so. All souls *eventually* move into greater states of consciousness.

As we raise our vibrations and ascend into higher levels of consciousness we may experience some discomfort emotionally, mentally and physically. We are transforming our dense lower vibrating carbon based cells into higher vibrating crystalline "light filled" cells. We are going through an alchemical process of body, mind and spirit. As we ascend, we transcend karma. Everything that is ready to be released will be brought up for review bringing about a change in our life experience. Old relationships, activities, jobs, belief systems, place of residence etc…may no longer serve your highest good. This is a positive experience and will result in tremendous personal growth even though it may be uncomfortable and chaotic at times. In order to ascend we must open ourselves up to change and step into a place of surrender and allowance. All discomfort is temporary! Eventually, everyone choosing to ascend into the higher states of consciousness will move into a state of health, harmony, joy, peace, spiritual abundance, full consciousness and unity consciousness.

Emotional Discomfort

1. Loss of identity. Feel like you are loosing yourself. Not feeling like you "fit in" anymore.

2. Dark Night of the Soul: As the old you dies (death of the ego) and you make room for the birth of the new you (Spiritual Self) you may experience an increase of chaos in your life. Your old ways just aren't working for you anymore! The sooner you can let go of the old and allow yourself to step into a new way of thinking and being the smoother your life will move. Depression, Grief, Sadness, Loss of Identity and Confusion are very common during the Dark Night of the Soul.

3. Your emotional body may experience upheaval during the cleansing process. One week you may experience Joy, Bliss and Elation and the next week you may experience Anger, Fear and Confusion. You may feel like something is wrong with you. This is part of the clearing process so please do not judge yourself.

4. Sudden extreme sensitivity to loud and crowded environments. While our energy bodies rapidly shift we will desire more time alone in our sacred space. Our connection to the Earth and nature deepens and we begin to experience the unification and universal flow of all living things.

5. Heightened desire to surround yourself around "like-minded" people and healthy relationships. You simply cannot tolerate low vibrational environments or toxic relationships any longer.

6. Irritability and Anxiety! Acceleration of time and not feeling like you can accomplish everything that needs to be done.

7. Feelings of despair and overwhelm. Our physical, emotional, mental and spiritual bodies are integrating higher vibrational energies from our God self. As we face God, we face ourselves! Things that need to be healed are being brought up to the surface for us to transcend. Previous behaviors and actions or karma   are being balanced at an accelerated rate. Our God self loves us unconditionally, but our misqualifed energy must be brought into balance….it can not be taken with us! Pulsating rhythms of our past are vibrating away and it affects how we feel.

8. Clumsiness, feeling out of sorts. Distracted.

9. Increase in psychic development and awareness. The ability to see beyond the veils may be emotionally disturbing if you are not accustomed to the truth of reality. These are natural abilities that will be returning to all of us

who are choosing to awaken and expand our consciousness. Be accepting of this process and do not resist. Work through your fears. We have earned the return of our spiritual gifts, welcome them! It may help you to find a group where you can talk about these experiences without anyone placing judgment on them. Some people have extreme fear of psychic abilities and some feel these abilities should never be discussed and should remain a secret. We are in the midst of planetary ascension! The truth is being revealed and we are returning to our divine inheritance and potential! It is time to share these experiences so we can reduce the trauma, shock and fear that occurs when people begin to experience the truth of reality.

Mental Discomfort

1. Our mind / ego / intellect will struggle to come to terms with the true nature of reality. It will try to cling to the old and not want to shift or change. Your mind may begin to panic as you experience the disintegration of your old reality. Blame, Anger, Fear and Frustration are very common.

2. Difficulty holding a clear thought….foggy thinking. Memory loss.

3. Communication difficulties. People do not seem to hear or understand you.

4. Mentally in high gear. Burn Out.

5. Obsessive need to understand what is happening.

6. Zoning out for long periods of time, not wanting to do anything.

Physical Discomfort

1. Intense electrical energy and heat that runs through the body. The body is being rewired to carry higher frequencies. Kundalini experiences.

2. Vertigo, Dizziness and Spaciness. A lot is going on in our brains! The right and left sides of the brain, our masculine and feminine energies, are being balanced and the pineal, pituitary and hypothalmus glands are being activated. We are also having a difficult time staying grounded because of the higher energies from the galactic center and our God self entering through the crown chakra. Daily "grounding" exercises and expanding and growing energetic "roots" out of our root chakra into the Earth will be helpful.

3. Intense Detoxification. As your body clears out toxins you may experience rashes, heat, itchiness, tingling or crawling sensations on the skin. The skin is our biggest elimination organ.

4. Detoxification may also produce pain in the hips, knees, muscles and joints and gastrointestinal disturbances as the body tries to rapidly release everything that is keeping it from reaching the higher vibrations.

5. High-pitched sounds and buzzing in the ear. An indication that you are raising your vibration and accessing higher dimensional aspects of yourself.

6. Hyper nervous system, panic attacks or anxiety attacks.

7. Heart palpitations. Our heart chakra is opening, activating and expanding. It must pump faster to accommodate the new energies coming from the galactic center and our God selves.

8. Back Pain. Our spine is being altered to handle higher frequencies and prepare for the raising of the kundalini energy.

9. Cranial pressure, headaches, neck and shoulder pain.

10. Bodily aches and pains. Our old cellular structure is dissolving giving birth to our crystalline structure. The body is being prepared to hold more light and a higher vibration. As we ascend, energy can get stuck in the etheric body creating blocks. Energy work, exercise, massage and hot Epsom salt baths will help. Also sun bathing helps burn off mucous and etheric blocks that naturally collect as our entire system transmutes all of its density into light.

11. Water retention. Our crystalline body requires more sodium chloride to ascend. Also our lymphatic system is being affected due to the rapid detoxification that is occurring. Drink additional water and exercise!

12. Disruptive sleep patterns.

13. Extreme Fatigue. Our physical and energetic bodies are growing and expanding. This requires an enormous amount of energy.

14. Flu-like symptoms.

15. Increased appetite and weight gain is common because it requires a tremendous amount of energy to transform our system. Also, the larger light body we have the larger our physical body may become in attempts to help us stay grounded.

Planetary Transformation

Every single person on Earth, at this time, was chosen by God to raise their vibration to their highest potential so they could participate in planetary ascension. Each one of us are "the chosen ones", who have the potential, to activate and integrate our Christ Consciousness and enter into the Golden Age. This opportunity comes around every 26,000 years for those souls who are ready to ascend into a higher vibration / dimension / reality. This is the time for total transformation and each of us must choose from our own free will to participate in this process. If we choose to resist this process our next opportunity for ascension will not be available for another 26,000 years. It is time for us to get real about the truth of our being and what is occurring in the Universe right now. The majority of humanity is suffering from amnesia, unknowingness and spiritual blindness. We have forgotten who we are and why we are here, but it is time for us to re-member. It is time for us to bring all of our parts or "members" back together and become whole once again. When we rediscover how extraordinary we truly are, all of our rules and distorted beliefs will begin to disappear and our spiritual abilities will be returned to us. This is the time of awakening to our highest soul's potential.

Everything has been set in motion and it is a privilege for us to be incarnated at this time to witness the fall of all old programming and paradigms that no longer serve humanity's highest good. We are birthing a new world, however, before we enter the Golden Age we must first go through the cleansing phase and release all negativity, fear, old beliefs, old behavioral patterns and systems that can not reside in the higher vibrating energy of the New Earth. Death and rebirth are natural cycles of change. We must first die to the old ways of being before we are able to birth a new way of being. Humanity and the Earth must go through their own personal cleansing and releasing of all discordant energies. Natural disasters are the Earth's way of throwing off the negative energy humanity has accumulated within the Earth's atmosphere (aura). She must also free herself of all lower vibrating energies so our arrival into the higher dimensions of the new Earth will be safe.

We are in the process of labor and delivery and there is always chaos before the birth of our magnificence. Each of us must set our intentions to be pro-active in our awakening process. We are spiritual beings having a human experience! In order to make it through this transformation with ease and grace we must connect up to our God self and bring our true spiritual essence down into our physical being. We must bring our spiritual self down into our body so the veil of amnesia can be removed from our consciousness. Once the veil is lifted, illusions will be exposed and the truth will be revealed. We must awaken to who we truly are and begin to live from our truth and not from the illusions of our egos. Being spiritual is not something we become; it is who we truly are. It is time for us to claim our sovereignty! We are divine, eternal spiritual beings….individuated, unique pieces of God energy!